Frozen in Time

Frozen in Time

Fossils of the United Kingdom
and Where to Find Them

Rhys Charles

First published in the United Kingdom in 2022 by Trapeze,
an imprint of The Orion Publishing Group Ltd
Carmelite House, 50 Victoria Embankment,
London EC4Y 0DZ

An Hachette UK company

1 3 5 7 9 10 8 6 4 2

The source for the Geographical Timeline is as follows: Cohen,
K.M., Finney, S.C., Gibbard, P.L. & Fan, J.-X. (2013; updated).
The ICS International Chronostratigraphic Chart. Episodes 36: 199–204.
https://stratigraphy.org/ICSchart/ChronostratChart2022-02.pdf

ISBN (Hardback): 978 1 409 19796 6
ISBN (eBook): 978 1 409 19797 3
ISBN (Audio): 978 1 398 70397 1

Printed in Great Britain by Clays Ltd, Elcograf, S.p.A

www.orionbooks.co.uk

Contents

Geological Timeline

ERA	PERIOD	EPOCH	APPROXIMATE NUMERICAL AGE
			present
	Quaternay	Holocene	
			11,700 years ago
		Pleistocene	
			2.6 million years ago
	Neogene	Pliocene	
			5.3 million years ago
Cenozoic		Miocene	
			23 million years ago
	Paleogene	Oligocene	
			34 million years ago
		Eocene	
			56 million years ago
		Paleocene	
			66 million years ago
	Cretaceous	Upper	
			101 million years ago
		Lower	
			145 million years ago
	Jurassic	Upper	
			164 million years ago
Mesozoic		Middle	
			174 million years ago
		Lower	
			200 million years ago
	Triassic	Upper	
			237 million years ago
		Middle	
			237 million years ago
		Lower	
			252 million years ago
	Pernian	Lopingian	
			260 million years ago
		Guadalupian	
			273 million years ago
		Cisuralian	
			299 million years ago
	Carboniferous	Pennsylvanian	
			323 million years ago
		Mississippian	
			359 million years ago
	Devonian	Upper	
			383 million years ago
		Middle	
			393 million years ago
		Lower	
			419 million years ago
Paleozoic	Silurian	Pridoli	
			423 million years ago
		Ludlow	
			427 million years ago
		Wenlock	
			433 million years ago
		Llandovery	
			444 million years ago
	Ordovician	Upper	
			458 million years ago
		Middle	
			470 million years ago
		Lower	
			485 million years ago
	Cambrian	Furongian	
			497 million years ago
		Miaolingian	
			509 million years ago
		Series 2	
			521 million years ago
		Terreneuvian	
			635 million years ago
Neo-Proterozoic	Ediacaran		
			720 million years ago
	Cryogenian		
			1000 million years ago
	Tonian		

There are a number of earlier eras which are beyond the scope of this book. Epochs in italics indicate unnamed units.

Introduction

Fossils provide a unique and fascinating look into the past, to glimpse a world that, whilst still our same planet, can seem truly alien. They tell a story of life across billions of years of earth history, and though we're used to seeing this in museums and documentaries, it's still surprising just how many chapters of that story can be discovered on the shores right on our doorsteps here in the United Kingdom; from dinosaur footprints on the rocky beaches of Scotland, signs of some of the earliest complex life in the Welsh black shales, to the giant ocean-dwelling reptiles in the rich marine realm of England's Jurassic Coast.

Major revelations in science are often thought of as experiments happening behind closed doors in laboratories, but what makes fossils so different is their accessibility. There are few other areas of science in which such breakthroughs can be made by a casual observer during a stroll on the beach, but this is precisely what fossil hunting can offer to the fields of palaeontology, geology, biology, and even climate science.

You don't need to have a PhD and access to masses of specialist equipment to potentially find great fossils. For such a small land mass, the UK is home to a surprising abundance and diversity of fossils, our country being as rich in ancient species as it is in accents. This includes those which are likely familiar, such as the intricate spiral shells of ammonites, but also those unlike anything alive today, like the saw-blade-resembling graptolites. And of course, there are that most famous group of extinct organisms, the dinosaurs, who also can be found here in Britain.

Taking us on a journey through the country, from the apex of Scotland to the south coast of England, we'll explore some of the more intriguing characters to have inhabited the area before us and go on a whirlwind tour of the major groupings of prehistoric life and how they all link together as part of a bigger global picture. Our journey through the rocks will take us through over half a billion years of evolution, across the eon of time called the Phanerozoic, a 540-million-year expanse of time which includes three constituent eras. The first, the Palaeozoic, stretches from 540 to 250 million years ago, and sees the rise of complex animal and plant life, including the origins of most the major animal groups we know today (such as insects, fish, and reptiles). The second is the Mesozoic, from 250 to 66 million years ago, best known as the age of the dinosaurs. Finally, there's the Cenozoic, from 66 million years ago to today, the time when mammals grew to dominate the earth.

Whilst places like the Jurassic Coast are famous for their geological history, it's easy to assume that there are no fossil hunting sites near you. By breaking down the country into fourteen distinct regions, all of them featuring multiple sites, this book aims to show you that there are fossils to be discovered everywhere. Whilst not every fossil hunt will end with finding something spectacular, rest assured that, armed with some basic knowledge on what to look for and how to go about finding fossils, even the most amateur fossil hunter will be equipped with the knowledge to unearth fascinating discoveries.

One of the best tricks with fossil hunting is to keep an eye out for the irregular. Fossils are commonly different colours and textures from their surrounding rocks, so on a beach dominated by grey stone, the flecks of black or white protruding outwards may be the sign of something important hidden inside. When the rocks are gritty like sand, the presence of smooth or reflective surfaces can be another sign that you've found something, a difference you can touch and feel as well as see.

Alternatively, it can be good to look for the all-too regular. Chunks of broken rock and cliff debris are usually without any particular form or shape, so it's unusual to see something that seems too perfect to have formed randomly. Spiral-shelled ammonites are a perfect example of this as they are so different in geometry from anything around them. Pattern spotting is a handy skill, as a single depression in the rock can be overlooked, but when a series emerge in a row, you may have discovered a trail of footprints.

We'll also explore some of the locations where the incredible geology of the country can be experienced, as well as places that may be quiet now, but have, in the past, been the epicentre for some of the biggest revolutions in science.

There is so much to uncover that, even as we embark on an exploration of all that is out there, waiting to be discovered, it is inevitable that some fossil types and names will be missed; something that will no doubt earn me some jabs from my palaeontologist colleagues, all of whom are certain beyond any doubt that the organisms they study are the most interesting and important to have ever lived.

There are also certain fossil types that crop up time and time again: brachiopods and bivalves, two names for groups of seashells. These regularly appear in the rock, looking much like their modern seashell counterparts, albeit made of stone. Often found as small rounded shapes of smooth, reflective rock, they can also be preserved as circular outlines, or even half-moon crescents if found in cross-section. These organisms, grouped together under the umbrella term of 'small shelly fossils' are by far the most commonly found fossils you're likely to encounter, their sheer numbers across time being so high, and those shells making them resilient and therefore more likely to survive as fossils, and easier to spot.

Similarly, there are many incomplete fragments of mysterious bones to be found, often stemming from long-extinct vertebrate animals. Such bones can be identified because they appear to be a regular shape in the otherwise irregular shape of a rock, like the thin curve of a rib, or the long, straight lines of limb bones. Though it can differ from location to location, bones like this can sometimes weather out to a honeycomb or fibrous texture, another trait to look for in the rock. The conical, peaked, triangular, or ridged shape of teeth are also common discoveries to be made. That said, geology can still throw curveballs with their deceptive mineral shapes, no more so than with something like a 'Beef rock', which occurs when the mineral calcite grows in fibrous lines which can resemble the look of a fossilised bone or shell.

One of the most exciting prospects when hunting for fossils is the knowledge that remarkable finds really can happen to anyone. Palaeontology is a science littered with tales of unbelievable discoveries made by people with little to no prior experience or knowledge of fossils, from a seven-year-old child hurling rocks into the sea only to stop because a particular stone looked funny, and then to report it and have it be a wing bone from a flying reptile, to people playing fetch with their dogs, who suddenly realise that they've been throwing around a small dinosaur femur. What is out there can amaze you, and anyone who is inspired to go looking has the potential to rewrite scientific history.

But before we hit the field, let's go over some of the basics.

Fossilisation

The word 'fossil' originates from the Latin 'fossilium', which means 'dug up' or 'excavated'. With this in mind, you could apply it to anything to have ever been dug up, but that is hardly scientific. There is no strict definition for what is and isn't a 'true fossil', but generally speaking, it is just a word used to refer to remains from the distant past – it's best not to get too worried with drawing lines in the sand.

A fossil is formed when an organism dies and is buried by sediments (like sands, muds and silts), whilst the soft body parts are normally either eaten or decay away. Over a very long time, this build-up of sediment is compressed into rock. Millions of years later, the rock and fossils are exposed to be found at the surface.

However, there is more to the story than this alone, as a fossil is not the same coming out of the ground as it was going in; it has changed substantially. If you have ever held a fossil or seen one, you will know that the original material that formed it (the organic matter of the organism) is long gone, decayed away, and the object is now made entirely of rock.

Commonly, this occurs as a result of mineralisation. After burial in the sediment, water percolates through the remains as the minerals dissolved within that water slowly precipitate out. This happens on a microscopic scale, preserving the finest details of the original organism. Essentially, if the feature was present when buried, it has the potential to be preserved. Frequently, this occurs with materials like silica and calcium carbonate which make up the chemical composition of most fossils, but it can happen with other minerals too, as we'll see later.

Another method of fossilisation is Direct Mineral Replacement, which commonly occurs in shelled organisms, such as the bivalves and gastropods of ancient seas. During this process, the original materials the shell was composed of (like the mineral aragonite) are replaced by more stable materials (like calcite). There's also carbonisation, which is common in plant fossils as we will see later.

Fossilisation takes a very long time, but not all 'fossils' have been fully fossilised. For example, Ice Age animals lived only a few thousand years ago, not the millions we tend to link to palaeontology, but we still call them fossils. Some research papers have even referred to bones only a few centuries old in this manner.

Fossilisation is a difficult process that is easily disrupted, whether by natural forces or other living creatures, and only a very small percentage of living things will successfully be preserved. It requires so many elements to be in order; a creature needs to have died in the right place, have their bodies not be overly disturbed, to be correctly buried, and held safely underground. It's difficult to fulfil all these conditions for even a single bone, let alone full skeletons, and the process is biased towards sturdier organisms, like those with hard shells and bony skeletons, and against creatures with soft bodies, like jellyfish.

Even having reached successful fossilisation, these extraordinary objects will then have to withstand millions of years inside the ground, often in dynamic conditions, thanks to tectonic movements such as colliding continents and plate boundaries dragging them into the depths of the earth, without being destroyed. They may be exposed and literally smashed back into sediment, or perhaps the opposite, in which they find themselves drifting too close to a tectonic plate boundary, crushed in the depths or by pressure and melted down into magma.

Finally, if they've made it to the modern day, they still need to rely on catching the eye of a passing fossil hunter who can recognise them for what they are. It would be an awful long way to come only to be stepped over or casually kicked back into the sea.

Despite all of this, fossils remain to be found almost everywhere, in astonishing abundance. The reason for this is quite simple: imagine all the animals alive today, and then imagine that number stretched across the vastness of time. Complex life has existed on this planet for over half a billion years. Suddenly, even that small percentage of organisms which are successfully fossilised add up to a huge observed number. To paraphrase a quote from comedian, writer and musician Tim Minchin: to call any one thing impossible is often to significantly underestimate the number of things that there are.

Fossil Types

Further to all of this, there are actually multiple 'types' of fossils. For the purposes of this book it is just the two main groupings that are important; body and trace.

Body fossils are what we most commonly think of when we imagine fossils. A body fossil is the term for the physical remains of the organisms themselves, even if fully re-mineralised. For example, a dinosaur bone is a body fossil, as are the spiral shells of ammonites, a group of extinct marine mollusc animals, or the fossilised leaves of plants.

If we're lucky enough to find multiple bones from a single specimen all preserved together in the position they would have been in during life, we call them 'articulated'. However, the majority will not be this neat, and the bones might well be in isolation or scattered all over the place. In this case, we would refer to them as 'disarticulated'.

By the nature of their very existence, animals can't help but alter the world around them. A dinosaur walking along the mud of an ancient riverbank will leave footprints behind and, if left undisturbed, these too can be preserved in the rock record and be formed into fossils. The animal itself is long gone, but that trace of its existence remains, hence the name given to such findings: trace fossils. Or, to use the original Greek word-root science so loves to adopt, ichnofossils.

Whilst trace fossils may at first seem a less exciting find than the flashier body fossils, trace fossils can be exceptionally useful, as they hold the secrets to reconstructing past behaviours of those creatures that lived before us. For example, the stride length of those footprints might tell us how fast the individual was walking. By measuring the distance between *T. rex* footprints found in 2016, it was estimated that its walking speed was around six kilometres per hour. If multiple sets of trackways are found then it can provide clues on social interactions, such as herding behaviour, seen in many herbivorous dinosaurs.

Footprints are amongst the most glamorous of trace fossils, though. Far more common are those often overlooked, like invertebrate burrowing traces, which are found almost everywhere. Often appearing as no more than wriggling lines of a different hue in the rock, I don't often reference their presence at sites in this book, but with a knowledge of what to look for, you will find them. These burrows frequently appear in limestones, where they most commonly look like pale (almost white) wriggling lines surrounded by grey rock.

The place in which trace and body fossils collide is where we get pathologies from. These are features on the body fossils which tell of behaviour. The most familiar of these are bite marks, still visible in long dead bones, but they could also be injuries, as when bone breaks it tends to grow back thicker than before. All evidence of past life is written in these fossils.

Other Terms

Three other things will come up frequently during this book:

Fossils are also not usually found scattered loose; instead, more often than not, you will find them embedded within the rock. In this case, we call the surrounding rock the 'matrix'.

Everyone has heard of the word 'species' before, but we will also be dealing with the word 'genus' a lot. The scientific names of living things are made up of two parts, genus and species – for example, *T. rex*. The first word, *Tyrannosaurus*, is the genus, whilst the second word, *rex*, is the species. Often people will know only the genus name but believe it to be the species. Everyone has heard of *Triceratops*, but how many know *T. horridus* or *T. prorsus*? These are the two species of *Triceratops*. Each genus can have multiple species within it, as different from each other as *Homo sapiens* and *Homo erectus*. Following standard scientific rules, the genus (singular – genera) will always be capitalised, the species not – with the whole name in italics.

When talking of fossils, we also speak a lot about things happening millions of years ago and, because it's somewhat annoying to write that each time, the scientific world has adopted the shorthand 'Ma'. So, if you see something written as 150Ma, that just means 150 million years ago.

Kit and Safety

Many people's perception of what a palaeontologist might need when out exploring the field is often far more excessive than the reality. When posing this question to the general public about what one might need when searching for fossils, answers can vary from the ordinary calls of a pickaxe and spade, to the extremes of dynamite and heavy farming equipment. As intrigued as I am to see how a combine harvester might fare sifting through fossils on the beach, the truth is that you really don't need very much at all to get you started.

Fossil hunting is an outdoor pursuit, and commonly involves scrambling over rocky, muddy and uneven terrain. With this in mind, the most important kit of all is good outdoor gear; sturdy boots, trousers and coats ready for all conditions. Palaeontology is certainly not for those who wish to stay spotlessly clean; if you want to really get into it at some sites, you may well end up covered in a fair percentage of the beach.

Luckily, most of the hard work of extraction has already been done for you by nature and the passage of time. The erosive processes of the sea, wind and rain break the fossil beds into more easily manageable chunks; boulders, pebbles, or (if you're lucky) a fossil that has popped out in its entirety.

All you really need for fossil hunting is a keen eye and patience. It's important not to lose heart if there are times when you come away having found little to nothing. It's an inevitability that happens to even the most seasoned of professionals with years of experience.

If you do want to use specialist kit, then a hammer is the common tool of choice, though it's important to make clear that I'm referring specifically to geological hammers. Using the regular DIY kind can sometimes be actively dangerous, as they're not at all designed for dealing with material as sturdy as rock and can splinter or even shatter. What you need is a solid geology hammer.

Every budding palaeontologist tends to gather a collection of hammers over the years, with a variety of sizes to deal with different rock types and sizes. You may even grow attached to yours, as I have to my own hammer of choice these past few years, which I've nicknamed 'Paper' for its uncanny ability to beat rock every time.

The use of a hammer does come with an additional caveat, however; eye protection is vital when hammering. When you smash into a rock, splinters can fly into the air, and the last thing you want is to have one of those end up in your eye.

I'd also highly recommend practising on less precious bits of rock before going to hammer the impressive specimens. Rocks can sometimes break unpredictably and it's best to hone your techniques on a few shelly fragments before you risk destroying your prized finds of the day (and this is something I say with bitter experience). Through time and practice, you'll learn the best places and ways in which to hit the rocks to have them fracture in the manner you're intending them to.

Hammers and chisels often have a 'smash and grab' feeling about them, but when it comes to some of the softer, thin-split shales, they aren't always right. Delicate fossils are best removed with careful use of a field knife.

As you gain experience, you might try to tackle the trickier heavyweight fossil challenges with mallets and crowbars, but these are at the extreme ends of the collector's spectrum (and only for those who don't mind looking incredibly suspicious walking along the beach).

Before moving on, we also need to have a few additional words about ensuring safety. Due to the way fossils are so often found, many of the localities in this book involve cliffs.

Needless to say, large towers of heavy rocks come with some fairly self-explanatory risks.

This is one of the most crucially important points with fossil-hunting safety; there really isn't much need to go too near the cliffs at all. The fossils may have originated from there, but the best fossils don't stick around, instead dropping down to the beach below. You are far more likely to find decent fossils in the shingle a good way away from the cliffs than you ever are from directly underneath them.

If you are working near the cliffs, it is also a good idea to have a hard hat on you. Small flecks of rock frequently come loose and tumble down the cliffs. These could cause nasty damage to an exposed head, but will usually bounce straight off a hard hat.

When it comes to coastal localities, the tide can also be a big concern. One of the most essential bits of information needed when exploring the coast is the daily tide times. Fossil hunting is a calming and therapeutic activity, one in which you can lose yourself for hours walking along the seashore, but if you don't keep an eye on the tide, you could well find yourself cut off. And if there's one thing guaranteed to ruin that good mood, it's having to call the RNLI after being marooned while chasing bivalves.

When to Go

One of the best things about fossil hunting is the fact that it makes the most of being outdoors, hence why it jumps to mind as the perfect activity for the best days of summer, with glorious blue skies, balmy temperatures and calm seas. Summer is certainly a good time to go, but there's far more to fossil hunting than that. What's truly wonderful about it is that there are few times it isn't worthwhile. Some weather that might ordinarily be considered bad can actually lead to the best conditions for finding fossils.

For millions of years, the fossils have been trapped in the rocks, and in order to become accessible to us, they must first be broken free. It requires quite a bit of strength to smash open a cliff face, and it isn't the kind of thing likely to occur on a calm summer's day. But when the weather is at its worst, with the rains and winds violently crashing against the coasts, that's when the cliffs get shaken up and scatter their fossils on the ground below.

We're constantly seeing storms turn over new secrets. Not long before I began writing this book, the news reported that winter storm Ciara had exposed a previously hidden and perfectly preserved dinosaur footprint set at Sandown on the Isle of Wight. Out of sight for over a hundred million years, it was suddenly revealed by just a few days of rough weather.

I should caveat this by saying that, naturally, a degree of common sense is necessary here. It is not wise to go out fossil hunting during the peaks of the storms, and the first priority should always be your safety. If the weather has any chance at all of putting you at risk, then it is best to stay sheltered until the worst is over.

The days after such storms have passed, however, are frequently the most productive times to go hunting, though again, it is still vital to be extra careful and steer particularly clear of cliffs, as they could be prone to collapse.

There are some cases where even a little rain can boost your chances of making a discovery. I personally prefer fossil hunting in light rain, as I find it often boosts the contrast in the colours of the rock. On a sunny day, a fossil-bearing rock might look grey all-over, but when wet in less-harsh lighting, the contrast between the grey matrix and white fossils within can become visible from a greater distance. This is obviously dependent on the site in question, but it's true for quite a few cases.

Seasonality has a big effect on success beyond just weather too. With coastlines being more prominent at certain intervals, like during spring tides, the waters can retreat further than normal, exposing new beds of rock which previously couldn't be reached; a rare extra opportunity for fossil searching.

Sites of Special Scientific Importance

One final thing to note is an acronym you'll come across a lot when exploring places for fossils: 'SSSI'. This stands for 'Site of Special Scientific Interest', and it is more than just a title, as these areas come with their own set of protective rules as well.

The single most important rule for our purposes is that, at an SSSI, you are not allowed to damage the *in-situ* formations. This means you're not allowed to hammer at the rocks still in the cliffs.

This rule does not apply to *ex-situ* material, meaning that which has fallen out of the cliff naturally. So, you can't dig into the rock of a cliff directly, but if you see a chunk of rock from the cliff lying on the beach, then you are completely free to break it open legally.

This isn't as big a setback as it might initially sound. As I've already said, you really don't need to spend much time close to cliffs anyway. Fossils are more likely to be found below the cliffs than in the cliff walls, and besides, hammering into the rock at the base of a cliff isn't a smart thing to attempt. It's not a good idea to tamper with the blocks at the base of a Jenga tower when that tower is over thirty metres tall and made of solid rock.

These rules are in place specifically to keep the fossils and people involved safe. If you do come across what could be the beginnings of an amazing specimen *in situ*, there is a process that you should follow. First, make note of or mark the location, enabling you to find it again, then contact either the relevant land authorities or local experts (museums or perhaps local geology groups) and report the find.

These groups will assess the discovery to determine if it is significant, and what to do next. This could be a full-scale excavation effort, or (much more likely) ensuring an eye is regularly kept on it to collect it as it slowly falls from the cliff, with it likely causing less harm to the fossil to let it erode out naturally.

If you are heading out to a site in Scotland, then you need to be aware that Scotland has its own set of rules regarding fossil hunting. I will not write them all out here, but they can be easily found online by looking up the 'Scottish Fossil Code'.

With the practical elements finished with, we can now start to explore some of the amazing fossil-hunting localities and discoveries these isles have to offer.

Northern Scotland

Lewisian Gneiss

The far north of Scotland can, in places, appear to be a remote and barren wilderness, one of the very few areas in the UK that looks to be largely untouched by human activity. It is perhaps unsurprising then that it is here in these ancient lands that you can find the very oldest rocks the UK has to offer. Strange though it may seem for a book on fossil-hunting sites, this first location does not contain any fossils whatsoever, but it does help to put everything that is to come into context.

Generally speaking, the underlying rocks of the UK follow a very loose pattern, which is that the oldest rocks are towards the north-west, and the youngest are in the south-east. It is far from a perfect correlation, as the dynamic nature of the earth means there are windows of older or younger rocks wherever you look. Nevertheless, that general trend is the pattern we will attempt to follow in this book, moving down the country, region by region, starting with the oldest rocks and moving south towards the more modern-day formations.

It doesn't get any older than the stunning rocks of the formation known as the Lewisian Gneiss. These rocks usually appear as dark grey in colour with bands of pink crystalline rock running through them like painted waves. Found around the Outer Hebrides, upper estimates suggest they may be an astonishing 3.1 billion years old.

It's an almost incomprehensibly huge number. To give you an idea of just how old these rocks are, it's worth considering that dinosaurs became extinct only 66 million years ago, putting dinosaurs like *T. rex* fifty times closer in time to us than the period in which these rocks were formed.

As the first word of the name suggests, this formation is named after where they were first described, on the Isle of Lewis, by John Macculoch in his 1819 works on the Western Scottish islands. There is no one single site where they can be best seen, as they pop up in various places in this region, notably in areas such as Mealista Beach. In fact, one of the best locations to see them is not on the island at all, but on the mainland at Scourie Bay. But what about the second half of the name, the word 'gneiss'?

A gneiss is a type of rock. If you cast your mind back to science and geography, you may remember the three main types of rock: igneous, sedimentary and metamorphic. Igneous rocks are those formed by volcanoes on the surface and magma deep within the earth. Sedimentary rocks are slowly laid down, grain by grain, over millions of years. Metamorphic are those same rocks that have been altered by heat and pressure to form something new. Those metamorphic rocks are further classified into 'grades' from low to high. A low-grade rock hasn't been altered a great deal, whereas a high-grade rock has changed significantly. A gneiss is just such a high-grade metamorphic rock, not far off becoming the next step of migmatite, in which the rock has actually begun to partially melt back into magma.

Essentially, these rocks have been through an almost literal hell. Under conditions of extreme heat and pressure, their chemical composition began to change; the very alignment of the elements composing their crystal structures changed. But the result can be quite beautiful, with wavy banding giving the rock an appearance similar to polished wood. These bands can be dark and black, grey and white, or even vibrant colours of rusted red and pink.

Astonishingly, though, their age is not the reason for their lack of fossils, as extremely ancient remains of single-celled organisms have been discovered from around this time. The oldest preserved structure upon which the scientific consensus agrees is a fossil that is 3.4 billion years old. Some even claim to have found specimens even older than these Lewisian rocks, going back to 3.8 billion years old.

Recent research led by Dr Holly Betts has suggested that life actually may have existed prior to 3.9 billion years ago. This would mean life was already on the planet during a particularly volatile time in Earth history known as the 'Late Heavy Bombardment', when the earth was being subjected to a prolonged attack from space debris.

The reason there are no fossils to be found here is not the age of these rocks, but rather because they are simply the wrong type. Fossils almost exclusively form in sedimentary rocks, such as limestones, sandstones, mudstones and shales. The extreme temperatures and pressures of metamorphism will almost always destroy any fossils. The only exceptions to this are in very low-grade metamorphic rocks, but even then, the fossils can be altered beyond recognition.

It might seem basic, but it is a fundamental lesson in fossil hunting: to ensure you are looking in the correct places. Igneous and metamorphic rocks will generally not yield fossil discoveries; if a rock is composed of angular crystals tightly bound together, as these are, then it's not going to contain fossils. If it is made of consolidated grains and sediment, such as sands and clays, then it could be worth investigating. Fossils require the sedimentary forms, the rocks laid down in beds at the bottom of the sea, in flowing rivers and lakes, or even in the sandy dunes of the deserts. It's a good idea to get acquainted with these types of rock, as you'll be dealing with them a lot when going into the field and looking for fossils.

The Lewisian Gneiss is in many ways an odd chapter to start this book on; not containing any fossils, and not even being restricted to one geographical area that can be discussed. But it serves to show the enormous potential scope of palaeontology, the vast amount of time life has been on earth, and helps put everything we are about to move onto into a geological context.

Caithness

From the oldest rocks in the land, we move to some of the northernmost, in the historic county of Caithness, home of one of Scotland's most significant geographical sites: John O'Groats. This is the farthest north point of the mainland of Great Britain; although there are higher points on the map still marked as the UK, this is the highest you can reach on foot without getting wet.

The geography isn't the only notable thing at John O'Groats, though – the rocks here do also have some potential for fossil hunting. The sandstones making up the shoreline here are a lot younger than the gneisses of Lewis, but they are still exceptionally old, dating back 385 million years, placing them in the Devonian period. Due to an explosion of diversity of one particular animal group at this time, the Devonian is frequently called the 'Age of Fish', and that's very apparent in the rocks here, as they are littered with fossilised fish scales.

Unfortunately, most of the discoveries here are a complete jumble. You may well find hundreds of the scales within the loose red scree, but they are scattered around like debris from an explosion. The odds of finding any more complete remains around John O'Groats are low. However, more detailed and well-preserved finds can be uncovered only a few miles to the west, on the beaches of the nearby town of Thurso, in a geological formation named for the location, the Caithness Flagstone Group.

All of the fish-bearing sites in this area were once a part of a giant body of fresh water called Lake Orcadie, which existed here during the Devonian period, the sediments preserving the fish that lived there. Many of the fossils from this lake are hidden today under the North Sea, but they can still be found in these Scottish exposures. The fish here are different from the ones we know of today, with many of them belonging to a group of armoured fish known as placoderms, which dominated the Devonian seas. These animals had thick armour plating extending from their heads to their pectoral fins (the horizontally orientated fins – or if you will, the fish equivalent of arms).

When considering this group, most jump to its most famous member, the monstrous five-metre-long predator *Dunkleosteus*. But this genus is known to be almost entirely from North America, so you are unlikely to find any remains like that here. The most common fish of Lake Orcadie is the much smaller genus *Homosteus*, recognisable from its flattened and rather box-shaped head. From its head shape, it was presumed to have lived near the seafloor, feeding on invertebrates, much like the catfish of today.

Complete specimens have been found preserved in large nodules of rock from Thurso, but, as with any great specimens in palaeontology, they are very rare, and you're much more likely to find scattered and disarticulated remains. But, if a nodule has washed out of the cliff, and you feel confident in your skills with a hammer, then it could be worth inspecting inside.

Thankfully, all the fossils here are quite easy to spot when they are exposed, thanks to the black and sometimes even reflective nature of many of the fish remains, contrasting with the light grey of the flagstones. The thin and relatively fragile layers of shale are easily split if the act of falling down the cliffs hasn't done the job for you.

Thurso's beaches are easy to access as being close to the town. The town itself has a classic sandy beach, but for the best chances of finding something of interest, you want to be on the east side of the river, where the land is dominated by agriculture and the coast made of flat rocks and low cliffs rather than sand.

Fish beds are common around Caithness, with a massive abundance of species having been discovered at the nearby Achanarras Quarry. A former working quarry (now publicly accessible), the spoil heaps here are still sometimes rotated by heavy machinery, bringing previously buried material to the surface and thereby refreshing the potential to find new fossils. Other placoderms are common here, such as the round-headed *Coccosteus*. More than fifteen fish species have been found here, including *Osteolepis*, a primitive lungfish ancestor on an evolutionary line closer to us.

Of the fossil sites at the very apex of the country, Thurso may be the most productive, and John O'Groats the most visited, but neither holds the title of the UK's northernmost fossil-hunting locality. To cross that particular venture off the bucket list, there are a few spots on the Shetland Islands to explore, with the best being at Exnaboe.

Within the siltstones here, you can find much the same as you do on the mainland: that familiar assemblage of Devonian fish, still part of the same ancient lake. Loose fragments packed with fish scales are common here, though usually without any form or structure.

If the kick of high-latitude fossiling is your thing and you really want to push this to the limits, then the Norwegian Svalbard Islands have plenty to offer by way of fossils. However, considering that the expert scientists who go there need to be trained to protect themselves from polar bear attacks, it may be best to give this one a miss.

Helmsdale

Travelling south of Thurso, tracking along the North Sea coast, you reach the coastal village of Helmsdale, renowned for salmon fishing. Although not many have heard of it, this stretch of Sutherland coast has long been hailed as one of Scotland's richest fossil-hunting localities.

The majority of the fossils here come from what is probably the most well-known geological period of them all, the Jurassic. Brought to the forefront of public science vocabulary thanks to the Jurassic Park franchise, we know this to be one of the three divisions of time during which dinosaurs ruled the earth (specifically the middle period, coming after the Triassic but before the Cretaceous – all three together making up the Mesozoic era).

A key difference between the Jurassic earth and today was the temperature, with a climate far warmer than that in which we live now. Aside from the effects this had on life at the time, it also meant sea levels were vastly different. During the Mesozoic era, there was no permafrost at the poles; the Arctic sea-ice expanses were non-existent, and Antarctica, today a frozen expanse of ice, was instead a continent covered in forests as dominated by life, including dinosaurs, as anywhere else.

Here in Britain, higher sea levels meant less land. During the age of dinosaurs, the name 'British Isles' was even more fitting, as the area was broken up into a series of smaller islands set in a shallow sea, with a climate much like the Caribbean. This wasn't entirely due to the atmosphere, but also our position on the planet, with continental drift meaning that Jurassic Britain was situated much farther south than it is today, at the edge of an ancient ocean called the Tethys.

The fossiliferous section of coast is along the eastern shore of Helmsdale, close enough to the village that you can easily walk to it along the rocky beaches. The Jurassic fossil shales can appear sporadically along the shore, with chunks of rock scattered all around. The only reason these rocks are accessible at all is due to a major geological fault that occurred towards the end of the Jurassic period, which brought these rocks back to the surface. This is one of those small windows of time that geology is full of; an oasis of fossils in a land where most of the rocks are ancient and igneous reminders of Scotland's volcanic past.

The rocks at Helmsdale preserve a marine ecosystem from around 145 million years ago. The best-known finds here are the 'Boulder Beds', so named after the large nodules of rock embedded within the finer mudstones. When broken open, these cannonball-like structures can yield some great fossils. As well as the boulders, Helmsdale is famous for huge fossil corals which can be found strewn across the beach. Recognisable from their distinctive pitted structure, these can easily be found lying loose in the mud. Other fossils can also be found in the dark shales, which yield bountiful marine invertebrate and fish remains.

There are other finds here that have brought Helmsdale more fame in Scottish palaeontology, and these are the reptiles that can be discovered. Although this group is not quite as common here as in localities to the south, it may be a good time to introduce one of the major players of the fossil world, the ichthyosaurs. Commonly up to three metres long, a body similar to a shark, the face of a dolphin with a particularly long snout, these creatures are icons of palaeontology, but are regularly mislabelled. If you want to really annoy a palaeontologist, call an ichthyosaur a dinosaur.

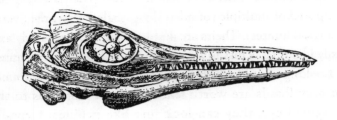

The skull of an Ichthyosaur

Ichthyosaurs belong to a group of reptiles specialised for life in the sea, which have the incredibly simple and self-explanatory name of 'marine reptiles'. They are emphatically *not* dinosaurs, nor are any other marine reptiles or pterosaurs (which we will cover later). Dinosaurs were a group of land-living reptiles, defined by a set of key characteristics (such as holding legs directly underneath their bodies, amongst many other features). Dinosaurs, marine reptiles and pterosaurs all evolved from the same ancestors in their long-distant past, but they were then separated by millions of years of evolution, making them uniquely different groups. As absurd as it would be to call a pigeon a crocodile, so too is it maddening for a palaeontologist to hear pop culture referring to these unique and amazing creatures as dinosaurs just because they lived at the same time. With that rant over, we can now get back to the fossils!

Ichthyosaurs are the most commonly found large vertebrate fossils in the UK. This abundance is mainly due to their long time-frame of existence, spanning more than 150 million years – from approximately 247 to 94 million years – and their habitat of shallow marine environments, making them prime candidates for fossilisation. They were clearly a very successful group of animals. Like all vertebrates, ichthyosaurs had spines composed of multiple rounded bones called vertebrae ('verts' to a fossil hunter). Theirs are amongst the most regularly and easily identifiable fossils you will discover of most vertebrates.

Looking a bit like hockey pucks when loose, these round, flat grey fossils are worth learning to recognise, as to the untrained eye, they can look just like pebbles. I vividly remember showing a vert to my father, who remarked he probably wouldn't have guessed its true identity and might have thrown it into the sea if he'd come across it because the shape looks ideal for skimming.

Verts come in different precise variations, but those of ichthyosaurs are quite distinct: usually close to evenly circular, the faces of both edges are concave (also seen in fossil fish verts). In life these would have had multiple extensions of bone, known as processes, attached, but these frequently broke away after death, leaving only the central core behind (leading to the hockey-puck comparison). If you do find intact and articulated verts, then take care as you may have come across a spectacular find.

Other commonly found sections of these marine reptiles are their ribs, which usually look like indistinct long bones and are fairly featureless. If you find something that is obviously a fossil from its colour contrast and smooth texture, and is long and thin with no clear features, the chances are that you have found a rib. If it's large enough, you might be lucky enough to see the curve or attachment, but it's more common to find fragmented middle sections.

The skulls of ichthyosaurs are notable for their large snouts (rostrums), filled with conical and ridged teeth, which would have been perfect for catching their prey (usually fish, cephalopods, or other marine reptiles). Unless articulated, skull material is harder to identify on site, as individual bones can appear like random chunks if you are unfamiliar with the skull anatomy.

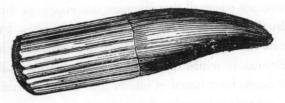

A single isolated tooth from an Ichthyosaur

On complete skeletons, you will see a supporting ring of bones within the skull where the eye would have sat in life: the sclerotic ring. Ichthyosaurs are the most frequent animals pictured with this feature, but it is found in a wide variety of creatures, including dinosaurs and many modern reptiles, even though their skulls are usually pictured as just having empty sockets. The four paddles (limbs) of ichthyosaurs are also distinct but we will look at these features in more details when we discuss other marine reptiles (for more information, see the section on Whitby, p.92).

Rhynie Chert

North-west of Aberdeen is the small village of Rhynie. With a population of under five hundred people, it's certainly not one of Scotland's largest settlements, but in the world of geology, it's a giant. The village gives its name to rocks hosting one of the most famous and best-preserved fossil collections ever uncovered, the Rhynie Chert.

A chert is predominantly composed of the mineral quartz, like a sandstone. What makes chert special is that the individual grains are so small that they are not visible to the naked eye. Usually dark in colour, with smooth surfaces, fractures can create razor-sharp edges. These have been used by humans for millennia, so whilst the term chert may be unfamiliar, you will no doubt have heard of one of the forms it takes: flint.

The microscopic scale of the grains that comprise these rocks is precisely what makes the fossils here so remarkable, as it allows the organisms to be preserved in incredible detail. There are countless fossil-bearing sites around the world, but in palaeontology, we have a word for the most impressive and important of these: the German term *Lagerstätte*, meaning sites of exceptional preservation. The UK has several of these, and Rhynie is the finest in Scotland.

When first discovered more than a century ago, the Rhynie Chert served to fill in one of the key moments in life history, telling us more than ever before about the time when plants first began to take root on land. This evolutionary innovation, of plant life moving from the marine ecosystem to the land, occurred during the Devonian and the fossils here are a little older than the Caithness fish at 408 million years old. The Rhynie Chert was formed by the activity of geothermal hot springs, comparable to Yellowstone or Rotorua today. These conditions, with rapid burial and preservation in silica-rich waters, are perfect for preserving fossils in fine detail.

As you might expect from such ancient species, the plants of the Rhynie Chert are all quite simple, with upwards growing and budding stems. They don't really appear much like any living plants, though they could be loosely compared to something like a glasswort.

On the surface, the fossils of the chert can actually look quite messy: random dark lines and shapes dotted around a grey matrix. You may not even think them fossils at first, just a smooth and splodged bit of rock. Where they really shine is under a microscope when sliced into sections. Features that we know of from plants today, like their tiny stomata used for air exchange, are visible in these species. One, *Aglaophyton*, has even been preserved in the act of releasing sperm cells.

Beyond the plants, one of the most common animal finds in the chert is the genus *Lepidocaris*, a member of an enormously diverse group: crustaceans. *Lepidocaris* was tiny (only half a centimetre) and somewhat shrimp-like in appearance. We will look at crustaceans in a little more detail at sites further south.

Before you get excited and pack your bags for Rhynie, however, there is one major drawback to this site. Most of the Rhynie Chert is locked out of reach beneath the surface. Various broken chunks of it have been known to find their way to the topsoil naturally but, for the most part, the chert is only known from specialist drilling and mining operations. It is not impossible that you'll find anything of interest whilst exploring yourself, but it is highly unlikely.

As well as guiding you out in the field to see and collect fossils for yourself, one of the most important factors of palaeontology is linking what you can find to the wider context of the history of life on earth. If this book contained references to every single place you could go to find a fossil, it would be exceptionally long, but it would also for the most part be referring only to small, shelly fragments. I've included a handful of 'extinct' or 'dormant' sites such as the Rhynie Chert for this reason. The fossils of the UK all make up one big story, and it's important to tell all of it. Of course, fossils can be beautiful by themselves, but it is how they fit into the grand scheme of palaeontology that makes them truly fascinating.

Isle of Skye

Whilst Helmsdale may have previously stood above its rivals when it came to the Mesozoic fossils of Scotland, a challenger has recently emerged. Over the past few years, in palaeontological news, the biggest discoveries in Scotland seem to be coming from the Isle of Skye.

In truth, this is far from a new trend, as the scientific importance of the island has been known for some time. The very first Scottish ichthyosaur (see pp.25–8 for full details) was found here in 1959, when fossil hunter Brian Shawcross found significant sections of the animal's body. But recent research has been shining a light on different animals, not only from their fossilised bones, but from what else they left behind. The story of Skye is largely told through trace fossils.

Staffin, to the north, takes its name from a Viking word for pillars, referring to the columns of basalt seen in the cliffs in this area, but along the coast at An Corran Beach, you find something entirely different. Along the flat beds of brown mudstone is a series of impressions with an unmistakable shape. Emanating from a central point are three elongated projections, making up the instantly recognisable shape of dinosaur footprints, made by animals walking over the soft mud in the Jurassic period, 166 million years ago.

Seeing as there are no skeletons to accompany the tracks, we can't say for certain what species made them, but the best theory is that they came from ornithopod dinosaurs. Ornithopods were herbivores, many of which showed specialised evolutions around their jaws, adapted for better chewing and processing of plant material, giving some members of the group the nickname, 'duck-billed dinosaurs'.

In total, you can see fifteen of these ornithopod footprints at An Corran, some of which reach up to fifty centimetres in length. But this is far from the only place on the island where you can find dinosaur trackways. It seems that, for the dinosaurs, the Isle of Skye was a very literal stomping ground, as research being led by Dr Steve Brusatte's group at the University of Edinburgh has recently revealed.

On the north-west side of the island, Duntulm Castle can be found standing in ruins atop a rise of red volcanic rock. The castle has not been in use for nearly 300 years, but in its shadow lies Score Bay and some far more ancient traces nearby.

The footprints here are much less distinctive than those at Staffin and, being tide-dependent, they are regularly covered up by water and seaweed. But, if you do see them, instead of the classic pronged shape, most of the impressions here are of basic circles, like mini-meteor craters, up to about seventy centimetres across. Similar such structures have also been found at Brother's Point.

These are some of the biggest footprints you can find in the UK, made by the group that contains the largest animals ever to walk the planet. In palaeontology we call them the sauropods, but you might well have grown up calling them the 'long-necked dinosaurs', and for good reason. Their exceptional necks would help them to gather food, either by sweeping and effectively clearing out the vegetation in front of them (like *Diplodocus*), or by reaching high to feed from the treetops (like *Brachiosaurus*).

Though we cannot say for certain what species of sauropod made these tracks, there are likely suspects identified from fossils at other sites. Chief amongst these is *Cetiosaurus*, thanks to a partial femur thought to be from a cetiosaur found near Valtos, not far from Staffin, in 1995.

Cetiosaurus was the first sauropod found in Britain, initially collected in Oxfordshire during the 1820s but not formally named until 1841. To date, it remains the most commonly discovered sauropod in the UK (although exactly how accurate some of those identifications are is debatable). It matches the time frame of the middle Jurassic period and it is estimated that these magnificent creatures reached about fifteen metres in length. Though this is still relatively small when compared to South American giants such as the *Argentinosaurus*, which stretched to more than thirty metres in length, as we discussed earlier, during the Jurassic period, the UK was a series of smaller islands, and therefore would have lacked the food resources necessary to sustain growth much bigger than the cetiosaurs.

Cetiosaurus bones have also been collected at quarries near Chipping Norton and Scarborough, and to get a true impression of the animal's size, you can see a full skeletal mount in the New Walk Museum of Leicester. *Cetiosaurus* currently holds its position as the second-largest dinosaur ever found in Britain, the largest being another sauropod, *Duriatitan*, though this is only currently known from a single humerus found on the Dorset coast. In the nearly 150 years since its discovery, we're still waiting on confirmation of any more material from this leviathan.

Sauropods weren't the only large herbivores on the island, as in 2020, a set of footprints were identified by palaeontologist Paige dePolo as probably being from dinosaurs from the stegosaur family. This is, of course, the family that contains the famous back-plated, spike-tailed *Stegosaurus*. The unknown relative on Skye could likely have grown to nine metres in length.

At the other end of the scale, Skye also formerly boasted the smallest-known dinosaur footprint, measuring 1.8 cm (around the same size as a blackbird footprint) and curiously nestled within a larger dinosaur footprint of a similar three-toed shape. A cast of this specimen is on display in the Staffin Dinosaur Museum). Although its crown was taken by an even smaller discovery in South Korea in 2018 (a one-centimetre print belonging to a dromaeosaur, a relative of the famous *Velociraptor*), it's still testament to the fact that dinosaurs weren't universally massive.

Skye does yield more than just footprints, however, as body fossils of animals can be discovered there too. In 2018, in the shale along the beaches on the western edge of the

Strathaird Peninsula, a team from the Natural History Museum uncovered the remains of a Jurassic turtle. A new species, it was named *Eileanchelys waldmani* and is important as, at 164 million years old, it is one of the very first turtles to make the move from land into water, the famous shelled reptiles having only first evolved in the Triassic era, about 50 million years earlier.

Having so far only discussed preserved animals from the land and sea, now we can add those from the skies too, as the remains of two pterosaurs have been announced from Skye. The pterosaurs were the flying reptiles of the Mesozoic, a group that includes the famed *Pterodactylus* and *Pteranodon*. As with the marine reptiles discussed on p.26, despite being reptiles living at the same time as dinosaurs, it is important to note they are not included in the grouping of dinosaur.

Research on one of these pterosaurs, led by PhD student Natalia Jagielska, revealed it to be the largest known pterosaur from the Jurassic period with a 2.5m wingspan. This giant was named *Dearc sgiathanach* in 2022, a Gaelic name for a Scots pterosaur. We'll look at pterosaurs in a little more depth with some other famous examples from the south coast (see p.213).

Skye is the centre of a Scottish palaeontological renaissance, and with new discoveries being made all the time, from different sites all over the island, there aren't many places in the UK as important in the story of British prehistory as here on Skye, and the beaches of Staffin, Brother's Point, Egol and Score Bay.

Southern Scotland

Siccar Point

Before delving into the fossil-rich locations in southern Scotland, it would be remiss not to mention another place of significance in the history of earth science. Siccar Point, on the Berwickshire coast, does not yield spectacular remains of long-dead organisms, but is instead evidence of an idea central to geology, without which we could not make sense of the rock around us at all.

During a boat trip in 1788, a local naturalist had his attention drawn to the layers of rock in this area. Horizontal beds of red sandstone lay near the breaking waves and sitting alongside them lay a sudden and striking change in both the composition and orientation of the rock. Thin bands of greywacke (another sandstone) ran at a vastly different angle, driving almost directly downwards into the earth.

The geologist was James Hutton, who would go on to earn his nickname as the 'Father of Geology' for his contributions to the fledgling science. Siccar Point would be the foundation of some of his most influential theories, leading some in the field today to have named it one of the most important geological sites anywhere.

The formation at Siccar Point was the first to be identified as containing an unconformity, but to understand what this really means, we must first learn about another theory Hutton proposed. Sedimentary rock beds are formed by sediments settling on the sea floor (or other environments), in a process known as deposition. Thanks to gravity, these beds tend to settle horizontally; invariably trending towards trying to create a flat, even surface. Bar a remarkable change in the laws of physics over time, it's safe to assume that this has always been true. The theory that the laws of rock formation in the past are the same as in the present is known as uniformitarianism.

Therefore, it stands to reason that if you see a bed which runs vertically rather than horizontally, then this inversion must have happened after the rock was formed. The sediment couldn't have been laid sideways, so it must have been flat first and later flipped by tectonic forces, such as those that built the highland mountains.

Even the toughest rocks aren't immune to damage, however, and over time, all are exposed to the processes of weathering and erosion. Whilst the forces underneath the earth's surface drive mountain building, those above actively try to wear them down. Imagine that, after being formed flat, a chunk of rock has been thrust above the surface, the horizontal beds now standing on end. Without further input from below, those erosive forces gradually chip away and remove the exposed rock until nothing is left at ground level, whilst the rest of the bed continues to run hidden underground.

If deposition were to begin again at this site, those new sediments, bound by the laws of gravity, will be laid flat. As they become rock, these new beds find themselves running at a vastly different angle from those beneath.

When looking at the entire unit, it would appear simply as lines of rock that happen to run into each other, but they represent a process that took millions of years to complete; a marker of lost time and a gap in the geological record across a period of extreme change. Structures such as these are therefore known as unconformities, and Siccar Point was the first to be identified as such.

Siccar Point began with the greywackes, the sediments of this dark sandstone deposited in the Silurian period, 430 million years ago. During the dramatic closing of an ancient ocean, as Scotland collided with the rest of Britain, the rocks were uplifted to an angle far beyond the horizontal and exposed at the surface. The red sandstones were then deposited here in the Devonian period, in a time of a more tropical climate. The time gap between the two is about 65 million years, a gap that is almost the equivalent of that between us and the dinosaurs.

These Devonian rocks are still 370 million years old, and in that time they themselves have been subject to erosion, but the unconformity can be seen today more or less the same as it was seen by Hutton when he formulated the theory 250 years ago.

Before achieving its legendary scientific status, the area around Siccar Point was used for mining construction materials, and the remains of greywacke buildings are still around, such as the nearby fort structure called a 'dun'. This mining activity ceased long ago, now leaving only ruins.

Easy enough to access by car, Siccar Point is a little under an hour away from Edinburgh, with some parking available towards signs for Pease Bay. It may not have been a fossil site, but these processes are important to understand. A basic grounding in geology skills helps any aspiring palaeontologist better understand how to read the rocks to discover fossils. But for those who perhaps may have found this pure geology a bit dry, then don't worry, it's time to look at more fossiliferous horizons.

Girvan

Even without any palaeontological experience, most people are familiar with many of the classic fossil types even if specific names aren't known; ammonites, seashells and dinosaur bones are all common mental images we hold when thinking of fossils. But life in the past was hugely diverse, and many creatures that once existed are unlike anything else we see today. Such is the case at Ardwell Bay near the burgh of Girvan.

Along the shore, the rocks here somewhat resemble the greywackes of Siccar Point: dark in colour and layered almost vertically, running down into the ground. But these beds are much thinner, with finer sediment, forming a complex and wavy surface. The rocks south of Girvan are not sandstones but siltstones.

These thin layered rocks are regularly split by natural erosion, with fragments found along the shore. Larger chunks of loose rock can be opened neatly and easily with a hammer. In some of these fragments you will find black flecks in the rock, each a few centimetres in length. They may not look like much, but they are the signature find of Ardwell Bay.

Looking closely at them, you can see they have jagged edges, like the teeth of wood saws. Each 'tooth' is known as a theca, and in life they were far from flat. In fact, their entire purpose relied on them having the correct three-dimensional structure. Each theca acted as a sort of cup, a hardened protective home for the soft-bodied creatures within. Together, they formed colonial structures called graptolites.

In this respect, graptolites lived a similar existence to today's corals. The individual organisms (zooids) would have had an appearance and way of life not entirely unlike coral polyps. Soft tentacle arms would have extended out from the skeleton to filter particles of food from the water. A key difference between them, though, is that while corals do this from a stationary base on the sea floor, graptolites would have freely floated through the water column, like modern plankton.

Though each zooid may have functioned like an individual, they each share certain features with the colony. Running one after another in a series, the theca form something akin to a rigid branch, a structure named a stipe. A true colonial organism, within this hard external skeleton, all the zooids were connected by an internal feature called a stolon.

Here at Ardwell Bay, the most commonly found graptolite fossils are of the genus *Orthograptus*, a type of which shows theca protruding in two directions off a single stipe. To reuse the same analogy, the fossil appears like the blade of a saw with teeth running along both edges. This isn't true of all graptolites, however, as they come in a variety of different forms, the stipes being a tell-tale way of recognising them. There is no one 'normal' orientation for the stipe, and we will look at this more when we later re-encounter graptolites (see St David's on p.131).

A graptolite showing four stipe 'arms'

These may not be the flashiest of discoveries, but graptolites are unique, and this makes them very useful in palaeontology as markers in time. They are a great example of what is called a 'zone fossil'. No single species of graptolites were around for a massively long time. This means that, without lab equipment, it is possible for scientists to date strata easily from the presence of particular graptolites.

Here at Ardwell Bay, the defining species is *Dicranograptus clingani*, placing the rocks into a zone of the same name. To put a number and more common name to this, they are around 450 million years old, dating from the Ordovician period. This actually makes them the oldest fossils we have yet encountered, though they are still billions of years younger than the Lewisian Gneiss (see p.17).

Despite the impressive age of these rocks, some of the familiar fossils of marine invertebrates were around during this period. The ever present smooth and rounded seashell fossil fragments and segmented arthropods (trilobites – seen more on p.114) are here; remains of animals living on the sea floor. The cone-shelled orthocones (relatives of squid with outer shells) which swam in the waters above are present too.

Though some are well-stocked, many fossil locations don't come with excellent transport links or parking facilities. The best way to access Ardwell Bay is to pull up at any small inlet where it is safe and legal to do so before walking a fair distance along the shoreline to the site. Thankfully, the road faithfully follows the coastline, making it difficult to get lost. Where the beach is dense with thin bands of folded grey rock, you will stand a better chance of finding graptolites than at any other location in Scotland.

Lady Burn

Without the erosive powers of the sea, there is naturally less exposure of rock away from the coast. Inland ground is usually covered by soil and vegetation, locking potential fossils underneath, hidden and out of reach. However, as water snakes its way through the land, it can remove this cover and expose the rocks beneath, meaning that inland fossil-hunting locations are regularly near rivers and streams, whether these are active or dried up. The occasional flash flood is all it takes to keep the foliage away and fossils exposed.

In the north of the UK, the word 'burn' is often applied to such channels where water carves out the land. When it comes to fossil hunting around these parts, the best of them is Lady Burn, only a few miles away from the graptolite site at Girvan.

The fossils of the burn also date to the Ordovician period; at 445 million years old, these are only a touch younger than the graptolite beds found at Ardwell Bay (see p.40). Also similar is the preservation, as Lady Burn is a marine environment in siltstone, but it is different from Ardwell in structure, as the rock is bulkier and as such layers are not so easy to split. Thin sheets aren't likely to be found here; instead, blocky chunks of rock are more frequently seen. This far back in time, the UK was well south of the equator, and a large section of Scotland still separate from Wales and England, though this gap was starting to close.

When it comes to the fossils themselves, Lady Burn is best known for its starfish beds. It's an example of a naming trend in geology that, while highly descriptive, does perhaps remove a bit of mystique as to the kind of fossils that can famously be found here.

Despite their name, starfish are not in fact any kind of fish at all. They're part of a completely different but majorly important group of organisms called echinoderms, marine invertebrates whose name means 'spiny skin'. This group includes familiar animals like sea urchins, sea cucumbers and sea lilies, as well as starfish. Echinoderms are often spoken about in palaeontology as they are enormously diverse, and their fossil record is substantial, being regularly preserved in marine sediments for half a billion years.

A typical Asteroidea starfish

The issues of nomenclature don't stop there, as what most of us think of collectively as starfish are in fact two very distinct groups of animals. Both groups can be found here at Lady Burn: the classical starfish group of Asteroidea, and the brittle stars, Ophiuroidea.

Though different, they share many similarities. Key amongst these are the body plans of both. Human beings, like all vertebrates, are bilateral animals, meaning we have only one line of symmetry, dividing us straight down the middle. Echinoderms like starfish have radial symmetry as adults, most commonly five-fold. It is a characteristic that has been present in the group since they first evolved in the Cambrian (more than 500 million years ago) and that they retain to this day. Symmetry is a common way of describing fossils for identification, so it is a good thing to bear in mind.

The structure of the arms is the clearest difference between the two types of starfish. Asteroidea are what most of us envision as the classic starfish, their arms having a wide base, tapering into five equal triangles when spread. Ophiuroidea, in contrast, have long and thin arms, looking like tentacles. It's easy to see where the name Brittle Stars originates, as they look far more delicate compared to Asteroidea. Both of these starfish varieties, Asteroidea and Ophiuroidea, can be found at Lady Burn.

It is rare to find a starfish whole, due to the fact that their mineralised skeleton often breaks apart and is dispersed after death, making them harder to find than the uniform shells of other invertebrates. What makes Lady Burn unique is the potential for finding complete starfish bodies, thanks to the rapid burial of the specimens before they could be broken apart, meaning that even minute details can be picked out in the rock. Even as fossils they're fragile, and extra care should be taken to avoid abrasions flaking them away.

They are far from the only species to be found in these rocks, as dozens of other marine invertebrate species are also here. Lady Burn can produce some spectacular trilobites and sea lilies, as well as the regular shelly fossils. They usually stick out as regular shapes in the otherwise amorphous rock, and can frequently have a slightly grey hue compared to the shaded yellow stone matrix.

There is a right of access issue with Lady Burn. So far, all the fossil-hunting localities I've mentioned in this book have been open, free to access for all at any time. However, Lady Burn is located on private land and permission must be obtained to enter the site. Being such a well-known location, the owners of the land are understanding of this and there is plenty of information online about how to correctly and responsibly gain access rights.

We'll be encountering more sites that need such special permissions as we go through this book and it's always worth looking up their individual requirements if you want to visit. These can change over time, so to write about any individual method of access in a book may only serve to outdate itself within a few months of publication.

Isle of Arran

Each year, the Isle of Arran is descended upon by hundreds of geologists, be they amateur, researchers or students. Visiting Arran, one of the largest Scottish islands, has become somewhat of a rite of passage for any student of earth sciences in the UK, with multiple universities and schools opting to take the trip across the Firth of Clyde. But why is Arran considered so special?

Aside from the draw of whisky heritage (Arran was once home to around fifty distilleries, though only one remains), it is the concentration of interesting geology that makes Arran so popular for pilgrimage. Described as a 'geologist's paradise' by Hamish Haswell-Smith in his extensive works on Scottish islands, Arran displays a whole host of different geological features compressed into one island.

The 'highlands' of the island are dominated by igneous and metamorphic rocks, due to a subterranean upwelling of magma to the north that took place about 50 million years ago, creating a large mass of igneous rock (mostly granite) underneath the surface, which geologists call a batholith. Other volcanic structures can be found across the island, which is scarred with channels of former magma (dykes), large bands of black rock snaking across the land like streams of stone cutting through the native rock, as well as the towering volcanic sill at Drumadoon Point, where pillars of grey rock erupt suddenly from the surrounding low hills of greenery and shingle beaches.

At Lochranza is found another of Hutton's original unconformities, as outlined on p.36 in Siccar Point. Here, vertically orientated grey metamorphic rocks from the Silurian period are overlain by a lighter-coloured Carboniferous sandstone, jutting out from the ground at 30 degrees to the horizontal. The connection where these two rock forms meet represents a time gap of a hundred million years.

But what about fossils? The most intriguing location in Arran is not somewhere you can go for traditional fossil hunting, but instead is a place where you can see one specific but spectacular fossil, one you certainly cannot take home with you.

Just about escaping the destructive reach of the batholith is the area of Laggan, just east of the northernmost tip of the island. Lying amongst the old remains of coal works and saltpans is a stretch of exposed sandstone. Believe it or not, this small patch of innocuous rock is the most famous fossil on the island.

Across the surface of the slab run two parallel lines of light impressions in the rock, slightly arcing in from the left (when facing them) before disappearing under the rock on the right. These curious lines don't run smoothly like train tracks but are composed of multiple indentations – like a dashed line. Again, we have found ourselves on a Scottish island discussing footprints, but these are far older than dinosaurs; dating to the Carboniferous period (320 million years ago), this trackway preserves a very different animal working its way through swampy muds.

The pattern of prints makes it clear that the creator of these footprints had many legs; many, many legs. They are near-identical to the traces left behind by modern millipedes, with one key difference: these tracks are 36 cm wide, meaning that is the distance between the prints made by the left feet and those on the right.

No body fossils were found with the tracks here, but a similar find in Canada in the 1850s (about ten years after the Arran track was first described by science) complete with body remains revealed the owner. The animal was indeed a millipede, but unlike those creatures we know today. This giant, named *Arthropleura*, was capable of growing almost two metres in length. Our Arran specimen would have been about one metre long, with twenty-six pairs of legs.

This extraordinarily large creature wasn't just a one-off experiment of nature; the species was far from alone in the leagues of giant 'creepy crawlies' of the age. Though the Carboniferous period saw some major evolutionary leaps, such as the rise of the first reptiles, its most infamous residents are these titanic arthropods. They included such names as the dragonfly *Meganeura*, with a wingspan the same as that of a pigeon. Even some amphibians went through evolutionary gigantism at this time, such as *Anthracosaurus*, a nearly three-metre-long predator whose remains have been found in the coal measures of Northumberland.

If the idea of giant arthropods makes you queasy, then you'll be relieved to know that these enormous creatures could never come about now. As we saw at Rhynie (see p.28), the period before the Carboniferous (the Devonian) was when the first true land plants began to take root on the otherwise barren land, and they really took off. Over the millions of years to follow, they diversified to well and truly take over the earth, to an extent they haven't managed since. Vast rainforests stretched around the globe, made up of giant ferns and horsetails the size of full trees (see Seaham and Whitehaven for more information on these plants – p. 66 and 79).

This forest domination had a profound effect on the earth's atmosphere. Plants grow through photosynthesis, emitting oxygen as a waste product, which we animals then use for our own respiration. This is an extreme simplification of the complex workings of the earth at the time, but the net result of all the trees that dominated the planet was that the Carboniferous had far more oxygen in the atmosphere. Today our air is about 21 per cent oxygen, but back then, it was as high as 35 per cent.

Arthropods don't breathe in the same way we do, by using lungs to inhale and exhale; instead, they breathe directly through small openings in their exoskeleton. This system means that their growth is restricted by the amount of oxygen in the air; if they grow too big, they will be unable to absorb enough to respire properly. However, if the limiting factor of oxygen availability were to be taken away, as was the case in the Carboniferous, it would allow them to evolve into much larger forms. Fully able to exploit the oxygen-rich air, some were limited only by the physical properties of their exoskeletons (they couldn't actually get larger or they'd be effectively crushed by the weight of their own bodies).

Aside from the lone trackway, there are a few other places to spot fossils on the island. On a hillside overlooking the southern shore of Corrie is a section of overhanging limestone covered entirely with domed structures, almost like very stunted stalactites.

The underside of this rock is preserving an assemblage of large brachiopods, with the slightly point-labouring name of *Gigantoproductus giganteus*. Also dating from the Carboniferous, though coming from the seas rather than the swamps this time, these animals likely lived and fed together in large groups on the sea floor. These animals feed by filtering food from the water with hair-like cilia and, by using their combined efforts and beating their cilia together, they could increase the water current flow and boost their feeding efficiency.

This impressive display is best viewed from the outside. When looking for fossils, it is best not to stand directly underneath several tonnes of overhanging rock. And, as should go without saying, a natural gallery as brilliant as this is off-limits for any disturbance. As with the trackway: look, but don't touch.

Nearer the water at Corrie, you might find some loose fragments of brachiopods or other marine invertebrates washing in, seen as small white and brown flecks of smooth and slightly reflective material in otherwise grey or red rocks, though as a whole the island isn't a profitable place for traditional beach-combing. As a showground and snapshot of deep time, however, the Isle of Arran is exceptional, and it's easy to see why so many aspiring earth scientists flock to this 167-square mile wonder of Scottish geology.

Northern Ireland

Larne and Whitepark Bay

It's a rather sad fact that, although the geology of Northern Ireland can be spectacular in places, one thing majorly lacking from this part of the world is fossils. Even now, during what could well be called a new 'golden age' of palaeontology, only two dinosaur bones have ever been found here. You read that correctly – not two skeletons, but rather, two individual bones. And none have ever been discovered in the neighbouring Republic of Ireland.

Both are very tentatively identified to have come from two animals we'll be looking at more closely later, in relation to more substantial discoveries: the nearly three-metre-tall, two-legged carnivore *Megalosaurus*, and the smaller but heavily armoured herbivore *Scelidosaurus*. Interestingly, both of the bones that were discovered here have come from similar positions: their hindlegs.

The rarity of these fossils isn't a fair reflection of the ecosystems of the island; it's due to the underlying geology. The rocks of Northern Ireland are dominated by igneous basalt, the classic black volcanic rock. And, for the record, there are no dinosaur remains from the Republic of Ireland because the vast majority of the sedimentary rocks there are from the Carboniferous, well before the dinosaurs evolved, leaving much of the island's geological history a mystery.

It's estimated that less than 1 per cent of the exposed rock layers (strata) in Northern Ireland is Mesozoic in age, but one place in that narrow window is at Larne, about a half-hour drive north along the coast from Belfast.

Whilst dinosaur bones aren't to be expected, this bay does contain rocks from a particularly famous geological formation, the Blue Lias. Named for its slight hue, this Jurassic rock series of alternating limestones and mudstones (dating back 199 million years) is common in coastal regions in the south-west of the UK, an area famed for a rich abundance of fossil material. Here in Larne, the rocks are less fortunate, though plenty of small marine shells can still be found, and even potentially ammonites.

The rocks do not originate from cliffs but are directly underfoot. As you walk along the beach, you can see the sequence change from orange and red sandstones of the late Triassic to the grey bands of the Jurassic Lias, where fossils can be found in loose boulders on the shore.

It might sound as though not too much can be found here, but there is promise and precedent for great finds. This section of coast was declared a Site of Special Scientific Interest (SSSI) in 1995 and, as if to vindicate this decision, just four years later it produced its best discovery to date, the skeleton of the 'Larne Sea Dragon'.

As is the case with just about anything labelled as a 'sea dragon', the bones belonged to a marine reptile, specifically an ichthyosaur. It was discovered by a student at Queen's University Belfast, first noticing a small protrusion of linked vertebrae peeking out of the rock. Careful excavation revealed the rest of the mostly disarticulated skeleton. These fossil-laden blocks can now be seen in the Ulster Museum.

A separate ichthyosaur skull was found further up the coast at Minnis North. Dubbed the 'Minnis Monster', it was actually found by a seven-year-old girl, Emma McIlroy, who went on to get a degree in Natural Sciences from Cambridge. This is a wonderful demonstration both of how you don't necessarily need expert skills to make amazing discoveries, and also of how fossils have the potential to inspire young minds to further explore the scientific world.

One of the few other places to expose Mesozoic rock appears to the north, at Whitepark Bay, and once again it shows fossils of two distinct periods. More Jurassic fossils can be found at the east cliffs, towards a collection of picturesque stacks standing out in the water. Some of these show eroded archways, with one having a distinct enough shape to have earned the moniker 'Elephant Rock'.

In the loose rocks are many of the same invertebrate fossils you can collect at Larne, but an abundance of flint has given the location archaeological significance as well, with evidence of flint tools and even clay figures thought to be several thousands of years old being discovered in the caves of the area, such as Portbradden.

The bay itself is a large stretch of open sand, representing a geological gap of about 100 million years; when the cliffs resume, they are far younger and very different from those on the other side. These rocks are from the Cretaceous, the final period of the Mesozoic, which saw the dinosaurs peak in diversity only to become extinct after an asteroid impact 66 million years ago. The strata of Whitepark Bay is younger than that cataclysm, about 90 million years old.

What makes these rocks stand out is their white colour; these chalk rocks are quite different from any other fossil-bearing rocks we've encountered thus far. Deposits like these are common in the Cretaceous and actually give the period its name, being derived from the Latin word for chalk. We'll look at how these cliffs form and what makes them so interesting at Danes Dyke in Yorkshire (see p.97).

Despite the clear contrast in the rocks and the massive age gap, the fossils you find in each are surprisingly similar, comprising mostly marine invertebrates of the same basic groups, mostly fragmented and eroded remains. The fossils are easier to spot on this side of the shore, usually showing up very clearly as black shapes contrasting highly with the white rock matrix. That said, many of the fossils are much easier to pick out in the chalk thanks to their highly contrasting black colouration.

Both Larne and Whitepark Bay are easy to reach; Larne in particular for being so close to the populous town. Whitepark Bay may not be so central but it's within easy walking distance of Portbradden, and there is a car park just above the beach. The sad odds are that you're unlikely to find spectacular fossils in Northern Ireland, but these two sites are amongst the best bet for them, and there is plenty of beautiful scenery to make the trips more than worthwhile.

Portrush

At Portrush, a small spit of land north of Coleraine, the jagged black-rock beaches look at first to be another example of that predominantly volcanic geology. But upon closer inspection you will see that there is more to these boulders than there first appears. When discussing the Lewisian Gneiss on p.19, I mentioned that, by the violent nature of their creation, a rock going through metamorphism tends to destroy any traces of fossils within it. Here in Portrush, some have survived.

Small white flecks of various marine invertebrates can be seen contrasting strongly against the black and grey surrounding matrix, and in some sections, clear ammonite patterns can be seen. They are not by any means beautifully preserved fossils, but the fact that they are there at all provides an interesting glance into the processes behind metamorphism and fossils.

These stubbornly undestroyed fossils have been known of in Portrush for a very long time, having been noted in scientific literature as early as 1799, before science even knew of the existence of dinosaurs, and when our best guess for the age of the earth was only a few thousand years.

Most importantly, this was twenty years prior to the idea of metamorphic rocks being widely accepted by geologists. Early scientists believed that the rock at Portrush could be basalt, and the very presence of fossils was used as evidence for an alternative, non-volcanic theory of how igneous material was formed.

The true reason for the fossil survival here is to do with their grade of metamorphism. The gneisses of Lewis were high grade, whereas these rocks at Portrush are low grade. They were not altered through burial deep within the earth, but from change much nearer the surface.

The fossils themselves are Jurassic in age, much like those at Larne, and would have been initially deposited in the same kind of mudstone sediment. However, millions of years later, once the fossils had been fully formed, locked in the rock, the surrounding area was intruded upon by a channel of magma under the surface. The fossils hadn't travelled nearly deep enough to undergo metamorphism, but suddenly those extreme temperatures were brought to them. Essentially, the mudstone and fossils within were baked until the magma finally cooled. In geology we call such an altered mudstone hornfels.

This was a dramatic event, known as contact metamorphism, with temperatures high enough to begin to change the nature of the rock, but not enough to destroy the fossils. The result was that this collection of fossils on the Northern Irish coast would puzzle early geologists for decades. You can find these rocks fairly easily, as the town runs alongside them, up the spit of headland jutting out into the water. On the west side of this is Portrush Harbour, and the fossils are in the rocks along the eastern side.

Being such a special location, though you are welcome to visit and observe the fossils, it is another site where you cannot take them away with you. Even if hammering into the rock were allowed, which it isn't, I would advise against it. Igneous and metamorphic rocks are far different and usually tougher than the easily split sedimentary. Attacking a tough crystalline rock with a fossil hammer is unpredictable and could be just as likely to break the head of your hammer as it is to break the rock. For both these reasons, this is one site, more than most others, where the rule is to observe but leave be.

Giant's Causeway

Whatever Northern Ireland may be lacking in fossil fame, it more than makes up for in another sector of earth science. Near the northern tip of the country, found along the coast between our previously discussed sites of Whitepark Bay and Portrush, can be found what is likely the most famous geological feature in the UK: the Giant's Causeway.

Recognised globally as a natural wonder, this 0.7km² site is composed entirely of pillars of grey rock, many of which have near-perfect hexagonal cross-sections. There are approximately forty thousand of them in total, some of which are twelve metres tall. We're used to natural processes creating unpredictable and erratic forms, like the sprawling branches of trees or the jagged edges of mountains, and it makes it hard to believe that these geometric columns could not be in any way man-made.

A clue that they haven't been sneakily constructed by the locals comes from the fact that this is far from the only place where similar structures can be found. There are examples of the same geology in Vietnam, California and Iceland, to name a few. These aren't even the only columns in the UK, as there are some in Scotland, within Fingal's Cave (on the Isle of Staffa). One thing all these formations have in common is the rock type they're made from: basalt.

A nickname regularly given to basalt is 'lava rock', and it is certainly an accurate description. Basalt is igneous, formed by volcanic processes; as lava cools, it solidifies into this black crystalline rock.

As with any such natural wonder, there is also a historical creation myth besides it. In this case, it is the story of a giant, Fionn mac Cumhail, attempting to build a land-crossing to Scotland. This is the origin of the names of both the Giant's Causeway and Fingal's Cave, said to be the intended endpoint of the land bridge.

The truth of how they came about is far more grounded, having to do with the physics of the lava cooling. As the liquid lava solidifies into the dense rock, it contracts and fractures into these hexagonal shapes. The longer it takes to cool, the larger the pillar formed is. Recent research from the University of Liverpool suggests that the temperature this would likely occur at was probably somewhere between 840 to 890°C, showing how relative the term 'cool' can be in the world of volcanology.

The causeway was formed during a period of intense volcanic activity in the North Atlantic around 60 million years ago, about halfway between now and when the ocean first started to grow. It was these same processes which created many of the igneous landforms we've seen already, such as those on Arran and Skye (see pp.46 and 31). It even had an effect further to the south, forming islands like Lundy, found between the coasts of Wales and Devon. This intense volcanic activity certainly did create some incredible geological features, though I hope my volcanologist friends can forgive us palaeontologists for holding just a small amount of bitterness for the fossils likely destroyed during this time.

The timing of this period, 60 million years ago, also means that it occurred just a few million years after the extinction of the dinosaurs, at the time when mammals were beginning to take over from the reptiles to become the new dominant animal group on the planet. The causeway was formed around the Paleocene or Eocene epochs.

As we discuss times closer to the modern day, it is common to refer to epochs. On the scale of geological time, an epoch is simply the division of time one step smaller than a period. Every period can be broken down into constituent epochs, but thus far, I have avoided doing so, so as not to overwhelm with even more confusing names to remember regarding time. However, once the Cretaceous comes to an end, it is more likely you'll be hearing epochs being discussed rather than periods.

The Giant's Causeway is one of Northern Ireland's biggest tourist attractions, and so it is obviously far from difficult to find and get to. Once there, you'll find plenty of additional information on the science and history of the site too. It may not yield you any fossils, but the geology is every bit as spectacular as a dinosaur skeleton.

North-East England

Howick

With the largest land area of the constituent countries, and huge sedimentary deposits far less disturbed by igneous intrusions than the others, it is somewhat inevitable that the country of England contains the richest abundance of fossil-hunting locations anywhere in the UK. As such, it has here been split into many regional sections, starting with the farthest north, right on the Scottish border, the north-east of England.

Facing outwards onto the North Sea, the coastline of Northumberland is rightly treasured for its beauty. It's hard not to be impressed by striking castles like Bamburgh dotted along this designated Area of Outstanding Natural Beauty (AONB), a classification created in the 1940s to protect such amazing sites in England and Wales, ensuring they remain safe from human development.

The English fossil-hunting locality we are exploring here is just south of Dunstanburgh Castle, on the coast of Howick. This village has already left a marked impression on British culture as being the birthplace of Earl Grey tea, but it is the rocks we're interested in, and they come from a period we've encountered before, the Carboniferous.

Previously, the giant millipede trackways of Arran (see p.48) revealed some land-living creatures of this time, such as the oversized arthropods and amphibians, but here in Howick you find remains both of terrestrial and marine life dating from around 340 million years ago. Fossils of ancient plants can be found here but are frequently locked away inside blocks of sandstone, which do not always split kindly. If you have the tools and feel confident enough, then the finds inside are very similar to those we will discuss at Seaham, the next site.

There's plenty of evidence of geological activity at Howick, with volcanic intrusions and a large fault system cutting through the exposed rock at the beach. But what we're interested in here are the fossils coming from the upper layers of limestone, those which preserve life from the Carboniferous sea. Alongside the familiar fossils of brachiopods and bivalves (commonly white or yellow shell fragments amongst the grey stone), you may well find curious shapes in the pebbles along the shore. It's usually far easier to find them in weathered smooth pebbles than fresh out of the strata, something which is true of just about anywhere these fossils can be found.

The pebbles are usually dark in colour but appear to be speckled with flecks of white. Closer inspection will reveal they have the distinctive shape of a ring, like a small Polo mint embedded in stone. Hardly ever found in isolation, it's likely that when you find one in a rock, there will in fact be dozens more in there. Each ring is not an individual organism but a single 'ossicle' (a small piece of calcified material), which, together with many more like it, form part of the skeleton of a bizarre animal called a crinoid.

Ossicles don't look much different in three dimensions than in two: a small flattened ring-disc. In life, they are stacked on top of each other to form a stem, rooted to the seabed by a spreading holdfast. At the top of this stem would be a mass of other skeletal components forming something like a cup, from which protruded feeding arms for gathering particles of food. Stuck in the ground with a stem and spreading branch-like arms at the top, crinoids may have been animals, but they share some passing resemblance to plants, hence their common name, sea lilies. They could also be said to look like a living feather duster, a trait which has given their stemless relatives the name of Feather Stars.

A crinoid showing a stem of ossicles, calyx head and feeding arms

This evolutionary design has clearly suited them well, as there are still more than 600 species alive in the seas today. Thought to have originated as early as the mid-Cambrian, they have been on the planet for an extraordinarily long time, leaving behind plenty of fossils to discover.

After death, the ligament tissue holding the stem together decays away rapidly, resulting in the individual ossicles being scattered loose. This is why it's so rare to find crinoids completely intact as they are in life. Even though finds of multiple ossicles associated together are common, intact bodies are not. The weathered pebbles containing jumbles of loose ossicles are by far and away the most likely crinoid discovery you will make.

The 'cup' at the top of the crinoid, known as the calyx, can appear to be a random fossil mass without the context of the stem or feeding arms. These sections, complete or otherwise, are more likely to be found in rock nodules here rather than neatly in pebbles, requiring a little more skill and time to carefully extract.

On first discovering crinoids, it's easy to think of them as being like sea anemones on sticks, but their true affinities are in fact with the same major grouping of animals as the starfish: they are echinoderms. This is demonstrated by the radial symmetry in their ossicles. Not always circular, some crinoid species have ossicles shaped like perfect little stars, making for extremely aesthetically pleasing little fossil discoveries.

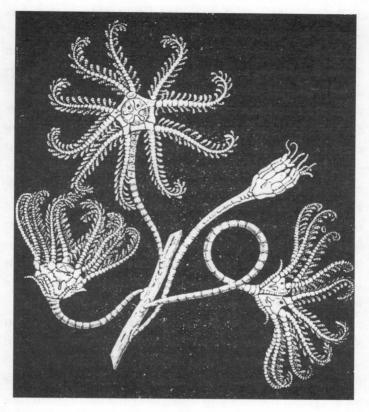

Several crinoids anchored to driftwood by their holdfasts

Other finds here include trilobites (the three-lobed invertebrates that resemble woodlice on the sea floor – for more detail, see Upper Gilwern p.114), several species of coral, and trace fossils. After years of exposure, slowly being eaten away by the water, it is sadly now difficult to see the light depressions in the rock not far from the beach entrance. These are Carboniferous footprints, but very different to those found on Arran. With rounded soles and stretching fingers, they belong to a vertebrate.

By this time in life's history, the arthropods were no longer alone in their discovery of the land; fish had, over millions of years, evolved their lobed fins into weight-bearing limbs, favoured primitive lungs over swim bladders, and had begun to climb out of the water. It's a remarkable story, far too complex and intricate to go into in much detail here, but the result was the dawn of the amphibians, and it is their footprints that can be spotted by the eagle-eyed at Howick. Specifically, they have been identified as likely being part of the amphibian group *Baropezia*, a general term for similar-looking trace fossils without a confirmed identity. But don't be disheartened to not find them, as they are not in an easily landmarked location, and barely visible even to those who know they are there.

There are roadside spaces available for parking in and near Howick, with signs guiding to the coastal path, which provides access to the rocky beach. The fossil-bearing locations stretch out from the long seaside bathing house to the sudden interruption in the beach by the large intrusion of volcanic rock called Cullernose Point. The best fossils aren't always abundant here, but more often than not you can find some intriguing pieces.

Seaham

In 2011, a dinosaur turned up in Sunderland, in a back garden no less. A man was digging up roots one day and unearthed a massive vertebra, identified as belonging to the herbivorous *Iguanodon*. Unfortunately, the bone he found was in total isolation, and with no strata nearby of the same age, one shouldn't get too excited about a possible dinosaur graveyard hidden under the city. This amazing, unexpected discovery was likely the result of a freak transportation long after fossilisation, be it by natural processes or even as a result of a human who brought the specimen north and lost it (perhaps whilst giving it a proper burial out of respect for our planet's long-dead former inhabitants).

Rather than rooting around in the back garden, your best chance of discovering the most interesting fossils near Sunderland require you to travel a little way south, along the coast just past Seaham. The town itself is home to a harbour and an extensive seafront defence of large boulders, but beyond this, the natural rocks are revealed up towards Nose's Point. From a car park here runs an easy route down to the fossils, and the interestingly named 'Chemical Beach'.

Thankfully, you needn't worry about toxic materials here – the name originates from the nearby Kipling & Co. Chemical and Iron Works, which processed materials for construction throughout the Industrial Revolution before being bought out in 1877 and closed not too long after. On a similar note, Seaham was also once home to a major bottle producer, one which dumped large amounts of glass waste into the water. This means that, as well as fossils, some of the most regular finds you can make here are of sea glass; beautiful, small fragments of Victorian glass worn smooth like a pebble.

The actual strata of Seaham dates to two different time periods; the lower grey rocks of the cliffs are from a Carboniferous environment like that of Howick (seen on p.61). The upper, brown-coloured rocks are from a period we've not yet encountered, the Permian, dating back about 260 million years. With mass extinctions and life beginning to evolve towards two of its most famous dynasties (the dinosaurs and mammals), this was a majorly important time period, but sadly, you are unlikely to discover anything much here from this period, other than bivalves. We'll look into the other groups and facts of this time elsewhere in the north-east.

By far the most prosperous fossil source at Seaham isn't natural at all; instead it's the fossils originating from a huge spoil heap left here after excavations of the nearby coal mines before their closure in the early 1990s. The rocks are quite distinct, slumping across the other strata they are darker in colour; a mass of loosely consolidated scree rather than the solid layering of natural cliffs. These rocks are also Carboniferous in age, but preserve a very different habitat.

Some of the most common fossils you will find here look like crocodile skin; or at least, that's certainly the usual theory put forward by children who have found them. Either that or they're hopeful to have uncovered some *T. rex* ecthyma. But these fossils do not come from any kind of animal at all; they are actually pieces of plant. The spoil heap is not marine. Instead, it preserves a swampy forest, part of the Carboniferous global rainforest systems that dominated the earth at this time, with the trees pumping the air full enough of oxygen to allow for giant arthropods like *Arthropleura* to evolve (see thro pp.48–50).

It's evident from the texture of these plant remains that the trees making up these ancient forests were nothing like those we see today. The trees we're familiar with, like oaks or pines, or even tropical kapoks and palms, were still millions of years away from evolving. Carboniferous forests were composed of tree ferns, horsetails and club mosses These plants still exist now, but whereas we're used to seeing them no more than knee height, 310 million years ago, their relatives could tower up to thirty metres into the air.

To sustain such massive growth, these trees had extensive root systems, which have preserved as those crocodile-skin-like fossils. (Although bark pieces also preserve, the remains of roots are more common here.) Having already been pre-buried in the earth, these pieces of trees have naturally boosted odds of making it through the long process of fossilisation, protected from some of the external forces which might otherwise destroy them.

One question that remains is what species of tree the particular section of root you may have found belongs to. This is trickier, as multiple species are known to have existed in this location but are often grouped under the same term: *Stigmaria*. This name serves as a 'form taxon', which means it is a generic term used to collectively described similar-looking fossils, even if they come from multiple species, much as we might use a generic term of 'fish' for a whole sea's worth of organisms. One of the most common genera here is *Lepidodendron*, which is colloquially known as the 'scale tree' due to that appearance of a surface overlapping diamond shapes, like lizard scales.

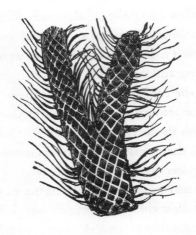

An example of a *Stigmaria* root structure

The vast majority of fossils here come out in small isolated fragments, but whole sections of tree have been discovered not too far away. The best of these was extracted from a quarry near the village of Stanhope (towards the Pennines) in 1915, when an entire base section of a giant *Sigillaria* tree was found. Whilst it may not tower as it once did, the expanse of splayed roots and remaining stump are still hugely impressive. Today, it stands for all to see in the yard of St Thomas's Church near the old quarry site.

Hunt Cliff

South of Hartlepool, where the River Tees meets the North Sea, sits a nature reserve known for its community of wading seabirds, beyond which run mostly level sands. These shores continue for a few kilometres to the town of Saltburn where, past the Victorian pier and water-powered funicular railway, the rust-coloured rock of Hunt Cliff rises quite dramatically.

In the spring and summer months, this stretch of coast is noisy with the calls from resident seabird colonies: kittiwakes, house martins and cormorants. By now, you should be familiar with the safety requirements of being near cliffs, but here more than most places, there's the added factor of bird droppings overhead to consider.

Topping out at more than three hundred feet in height, these are the tallest cliffs on the east coast of England; their reddish colour hinting at the industrial history of the area, as much of the strata is composed of ironstone. When iron is left outside, it rusts as a result of the metal reacting with oxygen in the air. This same principle of rust colouring applies to iron within sedimentary rocks, capable of giving vast expanses of strata a fairly vivid colouration even if only containing a small percentage of iron.

The ores mined here were processed in metalworks to be used in railway lines across the north, but here, we are looking past the economic applications of the rock to the fossils they contain, which predominantly date to the Early Jurassic, 185 million years ago. These rocks preserve a marine environment, a glimpse into the ancient shallow seas that dominated the country through most of the dinosaur age.

Perhaps the first thing you will notice about Hunt Cliff is how sheer it is. The sides are nearly vertical, and extra care must be taken, as high erosion rates mean that cliff falls are common and, from such steep and tall walls, very dangerous. Thankfully, sticking to the boulders and pebbles closer to the water line should provide more than enough opportunity for hunting fossils.

One of the more frequently occurring fossils here is something common in most Jurassic marine deposits. When first finding them, you'd be forgiven for thinking you'd stumbled across the weathered remnants of army surplus, as they hold more than a passing resemblance to bullets. Elongated cylinders tapering to a point at one end, and partially flattened at the other, you could believe them to be from World War Two. However, these finds are certainly not metal, and many are large and firmly embedded in rocks far older than the human species. These aren't human relics at all, nor, as was once believed, the physical remains of thunderbolts which rained from the sky; instead, these are fossils of an ancient squid-like animal, a belemnite.

Belemnites are not entirely dissimilar to their more famous relatives, the ammonites, both being extinct free-swimming cephalopods with tentacles for grabbing food. Originating in the Triassic, they too were unfortunate victims of the end-Cretaceous extinction, the asteroid strike that also saw the demise of the dinosaurs. They even moved in a similar way to ammonites, with both pumping water through a fleshy tube called a siphuncle, swimming by a kind of jet propulsion. Like modern squid, belemnites even had ink sacs, which can sometimes be seen preserved in some of the better specimens.

However, belemnites were not contained within a hard shell, like ammonites were, and were instead soft-bodied for the most part. The majority of what we find of them today are called guards, internal structures giving rigidity and balancing the animal. The thickness of these guards might also give clues about the animal's lifestyle, with thicker guards possibly belonging to belemnites that lived deeper in the seas. Despite its name, the guard would not have provided the animal protection, likely being little more than a toothpick for a hungry giant like an ichthyosaur.

Belemnites are exceptionally common fossils, and come in a variety of sizes. The smallest guards are thin enough that you could mistake them for sea urchin spines, whereas the largest is an incredible near-half a metre in length. That giant was discovered in Indonesia; here in the UK you'll likely find specimens comparable in length to your little finger.

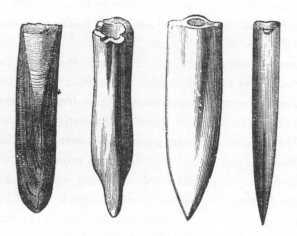

A selection of belemnite fossils showing
different guard morphologies

Like the stone columns of ancient civilisations, belemnites regularly fragment into short, cylindrical chunks, meaning the pointed apex of the guard is not guaranteed, and flat-ended pipe shapes are common. These 'pipes' are not hollow, though, and can often reveal a glimpse at the minerology of fossil interiors. Many fragments will show a white crystalline interior. These are called infillings and show places where minerals have slowly grown their crystals to fill the empty spaces as the animal has decayed, with the regular minerals of quartz and calcite responsible for giving them their shine.

Whilst there are plenty of fossils around Hunt Cliff, including the usual cast of shelly fragments, ammonites and crinoids, many of them are trapped in large boulders of well-consolidated rock. The belemnites are more likely to be found isolated than most of the fossils here, but uncovering other specimens may take some special skill with a hammer and chisel, so it isn't to be recommended unless you have some experience already.

This doesn't mean that the finds here aren't worth seeing, however, and some you'd never wish to hammer. As is some-times the case with marine sediments, there are some beds so full of shells, they form a near-unbroken surface of pure bivalves.

There have been some remarkable finds here too. In 2013, the scattered remains of an ichthyosaur estimated to have been 20 feet in length were discovered near these shores, so there may well be other impressive marine reptiles hidden out there. And if you aren't having any luck with uncovering fossils, you could always bring along some binoculars, train your eyes up and become an impromptu birder for the day.

County Durham

The Permian is a fairly underrepresented period of time, as far as British fossils are concerned. This is not due to the areas being unexplored or unreported, but simply because there aren't as many easily accessible sites where fossils from this period can be found by amateur hunters. However, the Permian is a pivotal time of earth history, and these fossils are undoubtedly an important part of the story of palaeontology in the UK, so it is certainly worth exploring here.

Some of the most recognisable animals of the Permian belong to a group named the pelycosaurs. Pretty much everyone has seen some reconstruction of *Dimetrodon*, one of the darlings of palaeontological pop culture: a sharp-toothed predator with a crocodile-like sprawling gait and a massive arched sail erupting from its back. An iconic silhouette, *Dimetrodon* and their relatives regularly find themselves included in lists and depictions of the age of dinosaurs. The problem with this is that they were not even close to dinosaurs, living millions of years before them. Like marine reptiles, they are prominent victims of everything in palaeontology being wrongly equated to dinosaurs.

The pelycosaurs were much more closely related to us than dinosaurs, despite the fact that they existed millions of years before them, as they were very early members of the evolutionary line leading to mammals. The purpose of their distinctive sails remains slightly mysterious, though the most agreed-upon theory is that they helped the animal better regulate body temperature, like a solar panel or cooling system. Though they were dominant in the Permian, only one genus has ever been found in the UK, *Ophiacodon*, discovered near Kenilworth in Warwickshire.

The north-east is home to the most globally known British Permian fossils, not land-living creatures at all, but remains of fish, beautifully preserved in a geological formation called the Marl Slate. Almost all of these specimens come from the working quarries of County Durham. Seeing as these mines are still in use and on private property, they cannot be accessed by amateur fossil hunters without specially granted permissions, although you may still come across examples of fossils labelled as coming from Durham in museums or fossil shops.

These fish are preserved in very fine-grained and magnesium-rich dolomite, as, despite the name, the marl isn't actually true slate at all. The bituminous composition of the rocks gives the fossils an almost black appearance, with incredible details visible. In some cases, even the soft body tissues of the fish have fossilised, showing details of the fins and other features that would usually decay away long before preservation (including some stomach contents, appearing mostly as dark black masses containing fish scales and teeth).

The rock type, colour and degree of preservation all serve to give indications about the original burial conditions of these fossils. These animals were buried quickly in anoxic conditions (anoxic simply meaning an area without oxygen – or at least very little). These fish weren't living in those anoxic layers at the sea floor, but swimming above it, before sinking down after death. Anoxia is important, as most decomposers, including microbes, require oxygen to respire; by taking the oxygen away, you remove many of the organisms that could break down or disturb the body. Combine this ideal setting with their rapid burial, and you've got an intact animal locked away, far more likely to be preserved in incredible detail.

By the Permian, the armoured placoderms featured in the Scottish Devonian locations, such as those featured on p.23, are long gone. The fish we find here instead belong to a group known as 'ray-finned fish'. This is the group that still dominate the seas of today; most of the species we associate with the word 'fish' fall within this huge group.

One of the most common fish found in the marl is the genus *Palaeoniscum*, which were about the size of modern mackerel. They're found alongside some of their predators, such as *Pygopterus*, which could grow to two metres in length, the barracuda equivalent of the time. In case there was any doubt they were predators, *Palaeoniscum* fossils have been found inside of *Pygopterus*, likely having been eaten shortly before the death of the larger fish.

As well as fish, there have been some other astonishing finds in the marl, such as *Coelurosauravus*, one of the earliest-known gliding reptiles, which used 'wings' that could be extended outwards from its sides. Only one such example of this species has ever been found in Britain, at a quarry near Hetton-le-Hole in 1979.

It's a shame more of the remnants from the Permian aren't exposed here, as it marks a truly transformative time in the history of life. At the start of this book, I mentioned that the eon of life is divided into three eras: the Palaeozoic, Mesozoic and Cenozoic. The Permian is the final period of the Palaeozoic, and if you're thinking that something big must have happened to warrant the changing of an era, you are correct. The Permian ends with the most catastrophic extinction event life has ever known.

In some areas, the Permian mass extinction wiped out as much as 96 per cent of life diversity. This was no asteroid impact, but instead the result of extensive climate change, caused by a multitude of reasons, including massive volcanic activity across Siberia. It's a fascinating subject, and one that we sadly don't have the space to explore more deeply here (or indeed much cause to, as the geological boundary between the two periods itself is not well preserved anywhere in the UK rock record). Thankfully, the topic is a veritable hotbed of research in the palaeontology world, and you don't need to look very far to find a wealth of information, should you be interested in learning more about this mass extinction.

The most amazing Permian fossils in the UK might currently be out of reach, but that is not to say that this won't change in the future. We live in a dynamic world, shaped both by nature and out own activities; it could be that one day a treasure trove of new Permian fossils is uncovered, allowing amateur fossil hunters to freely explore.

North-West England

Whitehaven

Fossil hunting is, for the most part, a relaxing activity to pursue as a hobby, one that can take you to beautiful locations and allow for leisurely exploration of an area. But there is one form of fossil collecting that is far from a leisurely pursuit. The gathering of this specific fossil type was, for a long time, the lifeblood of many parts of the UK, prominently in the north of England and Wales. These specimens fuelled a revolution more than two hundred years ago, changing the world for ever. I am, of course, talking about coal.

Coal is regarded by most as being no more than a black rock, different from others like basalt or obsidian only in that it happens to burn. But coal is not just an aggregate of abiotic minerals formed by volcanic action, it is the remains of formerly living plants. Under just the right circumstances, with enough time and pressure, this plant material becomes coal. The concentration of carbon within all of these plants is what gives the rock its black colour and combustible nature.

Not all buried plants are destined to become coal, however. Under different modes of preservation, they can keep their structures intact, still easily recognisable for what they once were to the naked eye. Some of these fossils can be incredible, appearing like artistic greyscale paintings of leaves in the rock, and one of the best places to find them is at Whitehaven, west of the Lake District.

Like Seaham, the most prosperous locality for hunting fossils here comes not directly from the cliff strata, but instead from the spoil heaps left behind by mining. The large scree slope of spoil towards Parton Bay is difficult and dangerous to climb, but the material is frequently washed out and scattered along the shore, so you can find plenty by beachcombing.

Plant fossils can be found loose, already exposed, or alternatively can be revealed by splitting shales, which tend to break quite forgivingly along the fossil surface. With its abundance of pre-broken shales, however, Whitehaven is a place where you don't need equipment to discover amazing fossils. Both the coal and definable fossils here are the remains of the giant Carboniferous forests; at about 307 million years old, the plant remains here are slightly younger than those at Seaham (p.66).

The rich diversity of the forests that once dominated the land is reflected in the fossils found here, as more than thirty different species of plant have been identified at this one location. Two of the most recognisable and frequently discovered are *Neuropteris* and *Annularia*. The former closely resembles a modern fern with rounded leaves, whereas the latter has sharper leaf blades which fan off in a circle from the stem, and is an extinct species of horsetail.

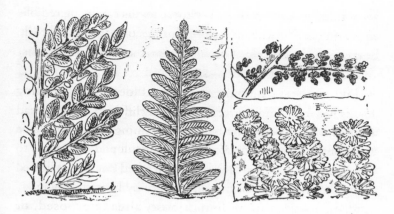

Various Carboniferous plant fossils showing *Neuropteris* (*left*) and *Annularia* (*right*)

You will find that, compared to many other fossils, those found here require very little preparation to get them to a display quality. Usually the simple act of carefully rubbing the mud and debris from the surface will suffice.

Being so close to the town of Whitehaven, this location is fairly easy to reach, with the most prosperous site within easy walking distance, following the beach to the right when facing the water. One thing to note here is the presence of a railway line, which brings with it some inherent risks. There is a tunnel underneath the line, which leads from the path on one side to the fossil beach on the other.

The reason that this geological marvel is so close to the town comes with a particular note of sadness in the historical context. Near to the start of the fossil shales can be found the former entrance to William Pit, site of one of the most notorious mining disasters the country has ever seen, when 104 workers were killed as a result of an explosion in 1947. Having experienced a host of accidents before closure in 1954, William Pit holds the reluctant title of being Britain's most dangerous mine.

Luckily, with the mine closed and no more chance of explosions, the site is no longer a risk to visitors in this regard. A memorial to the lives lost stands on the path, close to the walls of strata and shores, where today's collectors take part in the more peaceful gathering of fossilised plants.

This is the final Carboniferous plant fossil locality I will talk about in detail, but there are many more where similar finds can be made, as evidenced by Britain's much-lauded past with coal. Other localities where significant Carboniferous plant fossils can be uncovered include the Kent coalfield of Betteshanger and the spoil heaps of Writhlington in Somerset. Thankfully, the world is far less dependent on coal now than it was in the past, and we can finally begin to ease off that ironic situation of having the remains of a time famous for a high-oxygen atmosphere flooding our own with carbon dioxide.

Coniston

The Lake District is regarded as one of the most beautiful areas in the country, and one of the thirty-three to have been named by UNESCO as a World Heritage Site. As with so many natural wonders, the beauty owes itself to the underlying geology.

At the heart of this geology is a deep-set intrusion of igneous rock, similar to the structures underneath the Scottish Highlands. A huge bulb of granite has effectively swelled the ground above it, creating some of the tallest points in

England, including its highest peak, the 978-metre Scafell Pike. Locally, many of the peaks are known as 'fells', with the word adapted from Nordic use and meaning a high point of barren land, be it mountain, plateau or hilltop.

Even with igneous dominance, there remains plenty of softer sedimentary rocks, and this contrasting geology helps form the valleys in which the eponymous lakes of the region have formed. As glaciers carved through the land in the last Ice Age, they created the largest lake in England, Windermere, and the deepest, Wast Water.

Where sedimentary rocks are found, fossils often follow, owing to the ideal preservation settings these rocks offer, and the Lake District is no different. The most bountiful areas of this National Park are to be found west of Windermere, in the scree of the old quarries of Coniston. There are a few of these sites at the base of the 'Old Man of Coniston', which, it's worth pointing out, is the name of an 802-metre fell and not any particular local. All of them are a healthy trek away from the village itself, so be prepared to walk along hilly terrain (though odds are, if you've come to the Lake District you wouldn't be expecting any less).

In the past, this area was mined for copper and slate, and today many of the spoil heaps remain, with plenty of fossils scattered within them. Some of the quarry pits have since filled with water and become popular with swimmers; the former Banishead Quarry even has a striking waterfall at the northern tip of the scree. Another specific location touted by fossil hunters is the nearby Ashgill Quarry, but you can find fossils scattered around the foothills of the 'Old Man', not necessarily at any one point of the map.

The fossils here preserve a marine ecosystem that existed during the Ordovician (Silurian in some areas), making them the oldest fossils we discuss in the north of England, some dating to more than 460 million years ago. Trilobites and corals can be found in small blocks of broken rock you can pick up without extra effort, though some may be in larger boulders that may require a hammer. Often, the fossils don't contrast strongly with the grey of the limestone, so it can require some extra attention to detail to spot them.

As with most marine collections, common amongst them are the brachiopods. I've mentioned these animals many times already, as they, along with the bivalves, are easily the most frequent fossils you will come across anywhere.

Brachiopods and bivalves make up the 'seashell' fossils, coming in a variety of shapes and sizes, but they are most commonly seen as rounded structures of calcium carbonate, often with growth rings emanating outwards. Sometimes they have smooth shells, or they can possess strong ribbing.

However, this shape diversity runs deeper than just smooth or rough, as some brachiopods go beyond simple domes and have a shape like that of a butterfly; we even call the edges of these shells 'wings'. The point where their two shells meet is a great way to tell species apart, with some joining in a smooth unbroken line, and others wildly varying and offset, perhaps even zigzagging like corrugated metal. You can often find them in cross-section too, where they appear as thin crescents of minerals within the rock.

Bivalves are molluscs, the same phylum that contains cephalopods and snails (molluscs actually being the second-most diverse group of animals on earth after the arthropods). As their name suggests, they're composed of two valves, two bits of hard shell containing the soft body inside. Classic examples of today's bivalves are clams and mussels, and similar-looking species can be found in the fossil record.

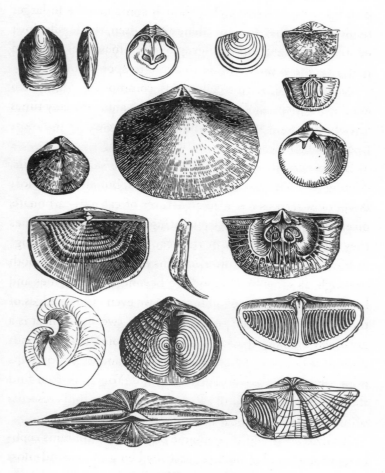

A range of brachiopod fossil morphologies

Brachiopods are not molluscs, but rather a phylum in and of themselves, their own unique group of animals. Even though they look very similar to bivalves (being shelled invertebrates), one of their key points of differences and the easiest way to distinguish them is their symmetry. Bivalves generally have two equal shells, the line of symmetry running between them, whereas brachiopod shells are uneven, one bigger than the other. The brachiopod line of symmetry is perpendicular to the shell opening.

There are plenty of other differences between them, but these are usually not as obvious. For example, their internal musculature is different, leading to variations in markings on their shell interiors, but being able to see this requires a degree of preservation you don't commonly come across.

As for why they're so ubiquitous in fossil hunting, it boils down to three main points. Firstly, they are common fossils due to being common in life. Both are hugely successful organisms, found in large numbers in bodies of water all around the world since their appearance in the Cambrian to today. Secondly, their shells are perfect candidates for fossilisation, being sturdy shapes of calcium carbonate. And finally, their mode of life is on the sea floor, sometimes pre-buried in the sediment, making their odds of fossilisation even higher. If dinosaurs were so obliging as to live half buried in the sea floor, we'd have a lot more fossils of them too, but alas.

Today, bivalves are still an incredibly diverse and common group of animals, but it's less good news for brachiopods. They took a major hit in that global catastrophe at the end of the Permian that we discussed on p.77, and although they also survive in the modern world (now commonly referred to as lamp shells), they never fully recovered their past glory. However, thanks to their sheer unavoidable abundance in the fossil record, it is certain that no palaeontologist will ever forget them.

Formby

When imagining fossil footprints, the minds of most will jump straight to the classic three-toed spread of a dinosaur, like those seen on Skye (see pp. 31–2). But they were far from the only animals to leave their steps behind in ancient muds. Some, like those found at Formby Point, just north of Liverpool, come from a far more recent past, from animals far more familiar to us, hoof and dog prints being some of the most immediately recognisable to be found here.

Today, Formby Point isn't wholly different from how it was when the tracks were created; that is, a sandy shoreline on the Irish Sea, with dramatic low-lying dunes extending towards the coastal meadows and forests. But what makes Formby special is when the tide pulls out, revealing flat plateaus of hardened sand preserving the shore surface exactly as it appeared 7000 years ago. The finds here are not only recent enough to be from a time when humans were in the area; *Homo sapiens* can be included on the list of species whose footprints are preserved.

Though we've covered great expanses of time already, this is something new. These fossils are within our current geological epoch, the Holocene. However, it should be made clear that this could change, as some scientists propose the establishment of a new epoch around this time. Dubbed the Anthropocene, it would describe the time during which human beings began to actively change the natural world around them.

Many of the Formby footprints will be familiar to those who've seen modern trackways of British wildlife, those of deer and wading birds amongst the most common. After all, being only a few thousand years ago, the ecosystem of Britain was largely the same, with most of the Ice Age fauna already extinct. However, the large dog prints found at Formby Point give a hint of something different, as these belong to the predatory wolves that once lived here in England, as they now do in the taiga forests of Northern Eurasia and America.

Of all the species who left their footprints on this muddy shore, one is consciously absent anywhere on earth today. They appear to be a pair of large exclamation points, very similar to the trackways left of deer and other hooved animals, a type of print known as 'slots'. With a length of 30 centimetres, these are from a substantially large animal, at least the size of a bull.

A bull is an apt comparison, as these footprints are from an Aurochs, a now-extinct species of cattle that could be found all over Europe and Asia at this time. In many ways, these animals were much the same as the cows of today, only slightly amped up. They were bigger, stockier, stronger, and had much larger horns.

The Aurochs may now be extinct (the last confirmed individual dying in Poland in 1627), but their legacy lives on, thanks to domestication. Whilst not full-blooded Aurochs, humans did breed the wild cattle with their own varieties for generations, leaving traces of Aurochs in certain breeds today. Perhaps the most recognisable are the Texas Long-horns, whose heavy builds and huge horns share unmistakable similarities with their wild past.

It's somewhat inevitable that, even with the traces of magnificent other animals on view, visitors at this site are so often drawn to the footprints identical to our own. We've all walked along sand and left footprints, and when we do, we don't often give thought to the idea that they might perhaps be preserved for thousands, potentially even millions of years, if the conditions are right.

The Formby footprints look as though they could have been made moments before you arrived, but they're baked solidly into the sand, preserving humans with a way of life very different from our own. Seven thousand years ago, humans as a species were in the early days of harnessing agricultural technology, only a few hundred years out from the classical hunter-gatherer lifestyle.

Now designated as a National Trust site, access to Formby is easy, with plentiful parking and public transportation options. The nature reserve along the dune system is today protected for the communities of red squirrels and Natterjack toads that find sanctuary there.

As with the other 'showcase' fossil locations, Formby is not a collecting site, and it is crucial that you show respect to the finds. Any disturbance of the footprints would be a crime, not only in the literal sense but simply a crime against science and decency. These tracks have survived for thousands of years, and provide a unique window for study of our own early settling days, at a place where archaeology and palaeontology meet. They must be protected.

Storeton Woods

Formby isn't the only site around Liverpool where prehistoric footprints have been discovered. A much older and far more mysterious trackway was found in Storton Woods of Birkenhead, where local stories persist of the 'Storeton dinosaur'.

This name is often banded around in the media when the subject of palaeontology in the north-west arises, but it is factually incorrect, although there was indeed a track found in the woods here, one from the Triassic period, when dinosaurs were rising to prominence, and it was certainly made by a large reptile, but not a dinosaur. The five-fingered, almost-hand-like print, is much better labelled as a pseudosuchian.

Keen palaeontologists will point out that I am splitting hairs here. As the name may suggest, the term of pseudosuchian applies to animals related to crocodiles, but beyond that, it is used as an umbrella term to include crocodiles, dinosaurs and even birds. However, the footprint here belongs to an earlier member of that group, very different from the more familiar descendants. So, it may not have been made by a true dinosaur, but it can be considered an evolutionary relative.

Crocodilians today are all rather alike to look at; water-living predators who keep low to the ground on their semi-sprawling legs. In the Triassic, though, the pseudosuchian ancestors were more diverse, including creatures like the armoured herbivores called aetosaurs, and the large prestosuchids that hunted them. Some of these animals were essentially doing what the dinosaurs would later become so famous for; that is, largely overshadowing these other animals of the past and leaving them in relative obscurity.

The Storeton track itself has been given a name, *Chirotherium*, which translates to mean 'Hand Animal'. As names go, it is quite vague, but there is a reason for this. Like the use of stigmaria for the roots seen in Seaham, on p.69, this is a placeholder taxon name describing not the animal itself but the style of track. Naming fossils like this is a common practice in palaeontology when there are no known body fossils of the animal responsible. For example, before the *Arthropleura* trackway of Arran was recognised as being from that giant millipede (see p.48), it was known only as *Diplichnites*.

Chirotherium as a name remains the only scientific moniker for the Storeton Woods track because, since the footprints were discovered in 1838, no other fossils have been found for whom the shoe fits. This is sadly likely due to the fact that the remains don't exist any more. The layer in which the prints were found is a red sandstone from a relatively dry terrestrial environment, far from ideal for fossilisation. This isn't to say it is impossible that anything substantial could preserve there, but it does make it highly unlikely.

Whether or not there are more prints out there, the original is certainly not. Having been professionally excavated out of the area, the various 'Storeton dinosaur' fossils are now on display in the World Museum in Liverpool and the Williamson Art Gallery in Birkenhead. In the woods, you can find artistic reconstructions of how the pseudosuchian would likely have appeared in life, as well as some of the sandstone outcrops in which the discovery was first made.

Yorkshire

Whitby

When it comes to fossil hunting in Yorkshire, one name will come up time and time again; the seaside town of Whitby. Long stretches of coastline either side of the town expose that most-loved of time periods: the Jurassic (185 million years ago). The shores of Whitby are quite possibly the richest fossil grounds in the whole north of England.

The cliffs that surround the town are mostly dark grey, composed of mudstones, with common falls leaving plenty of material to sift through on the beach. As many of the fossils are in the rocks near the tops of these cliffs, there really is no reason to stray too close to them, as all of the best finds will be amongst the shingle. Accessible from the town, you can walk west along the shore towards Sandsend Beach, or try out the various natural bay cuttings nearby, such as Runswick, or, to the east, Saltwick.

Tourists often flock here to find the most iconic fossils of all, those distinctively swirled ammonites. These extinct molluscs are part of the cephalopod group, like squid and belemnites, and would have had large eyes and tentacles protruding from their shells. A good way to describe them is to imagine a squid in a snail shell. Unlike snails, however, ammonites do not occupy the entire shell. Their bodies reside only in that final and largest chamber (the body chamber) whilst the others were filled with gases to maintain buoyancy in the water. We'll be mentioning ammonites a lot by nature of their frequent appearances and popularity, and I will explain more details about them as a group as we go on.

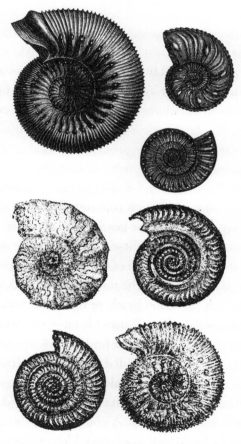

A selection of ammonite fossils showing their distinctive spiral shells

As we've seen previously, fossils can be found within nodules, lumps of rock with a differing geological composition from the surrounding bedrock, like the nucleus of a snowball. In most cases, the nodules are viewed more like 'the box it came in', but around here in particular they themselves can be impressive finds.

Nicknamed 'Golden Canonballs', these limestone nodules are highly rounded and coated in iron pyrite, better known as Fool's Gold. Whilst this material can get a little grubby and dulled by exposure to air and seawater, in good conditions it can shine as if made from solid gold. As if that weren't enough, these orbs (which can grow larger than tennis balls) can contain fossils, revealed by a good hit from a geological hammer – if you can bring yourself to take a hammer to such a gorgeous object, that is. Discoveries within them have included the ammonite genus *Eleganticeras*, which is a good name considering such opulent surroundings.

More frequently, nodules are dull in colour, but still easy enough to pick out from the regular broken fragments of rock along the shore. These large and rounded chunks may even have fossil edges protruding from them, the ridged texture of some ammonite shells being pretty unmistakable.

As always, when investigating, remember that hammering is a special skill, and it will take practice to get right and extract fossils neatly and safely. We've all accidentally destroyed material before, but with patience and care you'll get the hang of it. It's a skill that can't be learnt from a book, only by experimenting and learning how different rocks fracture hands-on, working out the best angles and hit-strengths to best exploit pre-existing lines of weakness in rocks, like those around fossils.

Like the boulder beds of Helmsdale (see p.25), when this strata is exposed, there are usually more than invertebrates to be on the lookout for, though these pieces are much more likely to be found amongst the shale than within nodules. Jurassic exposures may as well come with a warning of 'Here there be dragons', for incredible marine reptile remains have come from Whitby too. Having spoken of ichthyosaurs already, it's time to pay some attention to another big name of the group; the plesiosaurs.

If anything, plesiosaurs have an even more recognisable shape than ichthyosaurs, having gained notoriety as the base-model for the Loch Ness Monster myth. Their appearance is that of a large body with four elongated flippers, a stout tail, and extremely long neck, capped by a small head with sharp teeth. The overall look of Nessie isn't too far off the reality, though the same can't be said for the posture of swan-necking it is so often given.

As with the ichthyosaurs, the most common fossils of plesiosaurs to be found are vertebrae. There are a few tricks you can use to tell them apart; the plesiosaur verts are usually longer than those of ichthyosaurs, may not be concave at both ends, and have two small holes at the base.

Their flippers are also different, though they share an evolutionary solution to the problem of water travel. These marine reptiles evolved from crocodile-like animals, living on fish at the water's edge, eventually getting more suited to this aquatic lifestyle, to the point where they evolved to not have to leave the water at all. In order for the limbs of a land-dwelling reptile to adapt into a sea-going paddle, both ichthyosaurs and plesiosaurs increased the surface area by first massively reducing the length of the arm bones. Bones like the radius and ulna, long and thin in arms like ours, are very compact and stunted in marine reptiles.

Then, to make up the rest of the paddle, both have evolved hyperdactyly, which essentially means a multiplication of finger bones. Plesiosaurs and ichthyosaurs have far more phalanges (finger bones) than land-living reptiles, and to create the perfect paddle shape for maximum swimming efficiency they have basically 'filled out the space' with bone. In plesiosaurs, these bones look somewhat like our own, but ichthyosaurs have taken this to a further extreme, as their phalanges are reduced to be more rounded, like pebbles with straight edges. If you find a collection of these similar-looking bones all clustered together, you may well have found a paddle.

Part of the group called the Sauropterygia, another distinguishing feature is a thick mass of bone in the belly region, which, thanks to its rigidity, can also be preserved. The small heads of most plesiosaurs are less readily found than the sturdier remains of ichthyosaur skulls. This is something of a bitter point for me, having once found a distinctly headless plesiosaur specimen (though it did retain quite a lot of its neck).

Theories behind the length of these creature's necks vary, but the reason for it may have had something to do with their feeding on fish, in shoals and around reefs. It was unlikely to have offered much in the way of benefits to hydrodynamics. Some species, like *Elasmosaurus*, took this to ludicrous proportions with a neck measuring over 7m, containing 72 verts. Over the course of millions of years of evolution, reptiles can add more vertebrae to elongate their necks, a trait not shared by mammal lineages like giraffes which, despite their size, actually have only seven.

Whole skeletons of plesiosaurs have been found in the Whitby area, such as the large *Rhomaleosaurus*, now one of the most impressive mounts in the Marine Reptiles Hall of the Natural History Museum in London. However, overall finds of plesiosaurs are much rarer than those of their fellow marine reptiles the ichthyosaurs.

Other reptile remains from Whitby include ancient crocodiles, like the four-metre-long 'Snapper' *Mystriosaurus*, with a narrow gharial-like jaw, and even part of a sauropod, one of the oldest large dinosaurs discovered in the UK. The rocks from around Whitby preserve one of the most diverse and amazing assemblies of animals anywhere in the country. All such discoveries can begin with small bones that anyone can find on a casual walk down the Yorkshire coast.

Danes Dyke

Having seen so much of the Jurassic in other areas of the country, as we move south of Scarborough, we now encounter a decent exposure of that third period of the Mesozoic, the Cretaceous. This span of nearly 80 million years was when the dinosaurs reached their peak of diversity, only to slowly dwindle away, before being snuffed out completely after a massive asteroid impact near Chicxulub in Mexico 66 million years ago.

Even though this period is the time when the dinosaurs reached their most enormous sizes, our first substantial

Cretaceous site is in fact an excellent location to highlight some of the smaller animals of the age. The white chalk cliffs of Danes Dyke Nature Reserve are a fantastic place to find the fossil remains of one of the most primitive varieties of animal, around for over half a billion years; that is, the sponges.

Much like corals, sponges may not seem like animals, but they certainly are, just ones which haven't changed all too much since they first appeared at the base of our shared family tree. In the past, sponges even formed vast reef systems, with some specimens that can be found here even appearing somewhat horn-shaped, much like the rugose corals we will discuss at Caim (see p.105). However, the texture of these sponges will be different. Whilst corals have tough skeletons with visible growth lines, sponges (though still fossilised) have a more porous look, a particular dimpled nature.

A common variety of sponge here is *Siphonia*, which could be said to resemble a cartoon caveman's club, cylinders rounded at the top and tapering at the base, though you can also find them stunted, looking more like a puff-ball fungus.

At the very tip of the sponge is a circular opening which, in life, would have led to a hollow interior chamber of the animal. This shows how the sponges feed, then as now, like permeable chimneys. Individual cells beat their cilia (a hair-like structure), drawing in water. As it passes through their bodies, sponges filter out the nutrients they need and eject the rest out from the hole at the top. The sponge itself remains still but generates a current around it. This process can be dramatically revealed by using dye in the water around a living sponge.

In some cases, the chalk can form concretions around the fossils – look for round cream boulders in the rock, a few centimetres across – which will damage them if you aren't careful, and it is best not to strike a hammer blow too close to the fossil. You would be much better off giving it a wide berth and removing the surrounding rock slowly later on. It's more laborious, but it will lower the risk of fossil destruction.

Danes Dyke is just north of Bridlington, the chalk cliffs stretching along the southern edge of Flamborough Head. Fossils can be found all along the cliffs, though the best preserved are at Danes Dyke itself, getting less common as you proceed up the headland. The white colour of the chalk can make it surprisingly easy to spot fossils, but random concretions are also common, so you may be tricked more than once when walking on the beach.

There are plenty of other chalk fossil sites out there, the White Cliffs of Dover being one of the most famous geological landscapes in Britain. Nearby, there are also the Seven Sisters of East Sussex and Eastbourne. All of these places are Cretaceous in age, with similar fossil assemblages. Other regular invertebrates of chalk deposits like Danes Dyke and those of Sussex include belemnites, bivalves, bryozoans, crinoids and sea urchins.

Siphonia are far from the most abundant remains in these cliffs, however. It's literally impossible to visit Danes Dyke, or indeed any chalk locality, without seeing one organism in particular. They exist in incalculable numbers, yet many may never have heard of them.

A type of limestone, chalk is formed from the accumulation of lime mud on the sea floor, a substance which, in a slightly morbid twist, is composed largely of the decaying bodies of marine organisms. What separates chalk in particular from other limestones is that it is predominantly made up of a single type of unicellular algae, coccolithophores.

These photosynthetic organisms are still abundant today, part of the community we call phytoplankton, the sustaining force behind the marine food chain. Each individual is only 0.1mm in diameter, invisible to the naked eye. But when conditions are right, they can bloom, millions of them creating vast swirling patterns of bright milky-blue water, an ocean phenomenon visible from space.

Though unicellular, these organisms are covered in multiple plates of calcium carbonate; together they make up a shell called a 'test', and individually they are called coccoliths. They come in a variety of shapes, the most common being circular and slightly curved, like a plate. As the organism dies, these coccoliths sink to the ocean floor, building up to form the lime mud that, over millions of years, becomes chalk.

Being formed this way gives chalk its unusual properties. In geological terms, chalk is a very soft rock, hence why it was first utilised by humans as a writing implement. Those streaks it leaves behind are created by the rock shedding layers of fossil coccoliths and other lime-mud components. This habit of dusting off is so synonymous with this rock that it has become an adjective: 'chalky.'

Ironically, in recent history, this very chalky nature has made it less favourable. Today, most writing 'chalks' used on blackboards are actually made up of a gypsum-calcite composite that produces less dust (before they too were pushed aside for computer displays in classrooms, which remarkably don't seem to involve any dead algae at all).

Coccoliths are just one type of a myriad of different

microfossils, along with things like foraminfera, diatoms, and radiolarians. You might not have heard of these names before, but they are at the very forefront of climate science research, with analysis of their shells giving windows into climate records of the past. Sponges also aid in this, as they produce small, sharp structures called spicules, also common microfossils.

This is just another of those fascinating avenues of earth science that we are unable to delve into here, but is well worth looking up. Though often overshadowed by the more glamorous large-scale aspects of palaeontology, micropalaeontology is where many of the big, world-changing discoveries of this field are being made.

Mappleton

Many schoolchildren will have studied the incredible speed of erosion on the east coast of England during Geography lessons at school, using case studies on the rapidly retreating cliffs near Hull. The relatively soft stone in the cliffs combined with the regularly brutal conditions of the North Sea have resulted in England's east coast being one of the fastest eroding areas in Europe.

This rapid erosion has led to some fantastic landform features, such as the extraordinary spit of land, Spurn Point, in the Humber Estuary. This is fantastic for fossil hunting, as this erosion means that fossils are constantly falling out of the cliffs, but, as these are a continuation of a violent and dynamic system, what you may find here doesn't always make sense.

The beaches of Mappleton are a classic example. The strata here are far younger than the Mesozoic rocks of Whitby or Danes Dyke (see pp.92 and 97), dating instead to the Pleistocene epoch. The material that can be found here was deposited within the last hundred thousand years, in a period of time commonly referred to as the Ice Age. This history provides the key to understanding the site.

Although these cliffs are less than a million years old, it's common for you to discover fossils here that are far older than the cliffs themselves. Belemnites, ammonites, and even ichthyosaur teeth have turned up, all of which went extinct at the end of the Mesozoic. Corals from the Carboniferous can even be found here, though this is a rarity.

There are certainly examples out there of species being dis-covered to have lived on well past their presumed extinction. The most famous example of this is the coelacanth, a fish believed to have died out with the dinosaurs and known only from fossils until 1938, when South African museum worker, Marjorie Courtenay-Latimer, found a freshly caught one in a local fish market. We now know there's a population of these fish surviving in the Western Indian ocean. In palaeontology, we call such organisms 'Lazarus taxa.' However, the evidence of such ancient species at Mappleton is not due to this.

Instead, the reason for this can be found by looking at the *in-situ* strata themselves. The rocks here are boulder clays, created by the activity of a glacier, vast sheets of ice that dominated the Northern Hemisphere in the Ice Age. In the UK, they covered much of Scotland and Northern England, stretching towards the Bristol Channel through Wales and extending far along the east coast of England.

Glaciers are impressive forces of nature. When a multi-thousand-tonne block of ice begins to travel across the land, small patches of relatively soft sedimentary rocks do not have the power to stop it. Instead, the glacier carves through them, picking up chunks and mixing them with the ice and earth. As the glacier moves to enter warmer conditions, it melts away, and whatever material is picked up is deposited down again, forming boulder clays. This includes all of that material which has been transported miles from where it initially lay. We call these migratory rocks erratics, and they are the source of the 'alien' fossils that can be found at Mappleton.

Like a television clip show, Mappleton is a mash-up of fossils sourced from the strata to the north. The boulder clay itself is very soft (contributing to that fast coastal erosion), but the fossil-bearing rocks are the solid blocks which tumble out of it, many of which are limestone nodules.

Being such a strange collection of fossils, it is hard to predict what you are likely to find, but there should be plenty out there to be discovered. The cliffs are weathered away so quickly that new material is constantly appearing on the beach. A clear warning here then is that special care should be taken nearby any cliff for which the speed of its collapse is the major talking point. By its very nature, boulder clay can be quite messy to deal with, so you can expect to get your hands muddy when extracting fossils here, as many of them may be within masses of soft clay. And be wary of the potential danger of getting literally stuck in!

The site is easy enough to access, being only a half-hour drive north-east from the centre of Hull, with a car park above the main beach access. The village itself has convenient transport options too. Once down on the shoreline, the cliffs stretch in both directions and you should be able to find material in the shore debris quite easily. As always, remember to check the tide times carefully as that is one of the easier things to predict at this erratically bizarre fossil locality.

North and Mid Wales

Caim

The north of Wales is usually associated with the mountains and valleys of Snowdonia, but before we reach them on our journey south is a different landscape altogether, separated from the rest of the country by the Menai Strait. This is the Isle of Anglesey and is our first stop in this fourth and final constituent country of the UK as we continue south.

This island, the largest by area in the Irish Sea, has no shortage of interesting landmarks. Connected to the mainland by the historic Menai and Britannia bridges, it also hosts the village of Llanfairpwyllgwyngyllgogerychwyrndrobwllllantysiliogogogoch, which is perhaps unsurprisingly, the longest place name in Europe and the second-longest official one-word place name in the world, although it is believed that this impressively lengthy name was invented for promotional purposes. When it comes to fossils, however, the one site on the island to stand out is on the eastern tip, near an area called Caim.

Here, the rocks are Carboniferous in age (340 million years old) and are once again marine limestones. These are extensive reef systems but, just as the forests were made up of surprisingly alien species during this period, the reefs were also far different from what we know today.

Reefs in the tropical seas of our world today show an astonishing diversity of animal life; a vibrant and unique community of shapes, sizes and colours. However, despite the variety of appearances, every single living species of stony coral belongs to the same order of animals, the Scleractinia. This wasn't always the case, however, as the fossil record shows three distinct orders, including two extinct varieties known as rugose and tabulate corals.

Particularly easy to identify are the rugose corals, thanks to one of their most common morphs being a distinctive horn shape, which also gives them their common nickname of 'horn corals'. Imagine the shape of a rhinoceros or *Triceratops* horn on its own, then invert it so that the thinner point is down and the thick base pointing up; this is the basic shape of a classic rugose. Another giveaway when looking for these corals is the cross-section, which will show lines running inwards, like the spokes of a bicycle wheel. The coral will likely show lines running on the outside, both vertically from the point upwards, and in growth rings perpendicular to this.

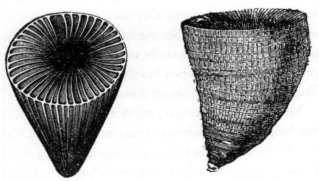

Individual rugose horn corals, seen in top and side views

The thick top of the horn is the place where, in life, the coral polyp would protrude. Just like modern corals, the hard structure is their mineralised skeleton, with the real living element being a soft-bodied little thing with tentacles extended into the water to catch food. All orders of corals belong to the same phyla of animal, a group that also includes the jellyfish and anemones. All the members of this group use the stinging cells in their fleshy tentacle-like arms to gather food. This feature has given this major animal group their scientific name, the cnidarians (coming from the Greek word for 'stinging nettle').

Most rugose corals are colonial, meaning that if you do find a fossilised one, it is likely that you'll see it surrounded by others. It's frequently harder to find one solitary coral than a whole community of them.

Amongst the most common genus at Caim is *Lithostrotion*, a small and successful coral that regularly appears in Carboniferous limestones. Although they retain the circular cross-section, they are more elongated than the classic horn, so may appear (in the lateral view) more like a bundle of sticks made of stone (much like another genus here, *Siphonodendron*). In top-down orientation, they can look like circular pits in rock with those spoke-like structures giving them away. The larger specimens, which can be in isolation, will likely be of the genus *Caninia*. Even when heavily weathered, certain features like their overall horn shape should still be recognisable.

More than just corals, other reef inhabitants like the brachiopods and bivalves can also be found at Caim. But the best finds remain the rugose corals, with certain layers of the headland densely packed with them. Chunks of these layers regularly break away and litter the beach.

The best fossiling area of Caim isn't particularly easy to reach and involves a hefty amount of walking. It is so easy to get lost whilst trying to figure out a more direct route to a site, and so in this case, it is worth following a longer but simpler route. This is to travel to the tip of the headland, near the black and white lighthouse at Penmon (which itself sits on a stretch of dark limestone). From here, coastal paths allow you to follow the north-facing coast to reach the boulder-strewn shores.

However successful the rugose and tabulate corals may once have been, they were ultimately doomed. Like so many others, they were victims of the great Permian extinction event that we saw on p.77. Scleractinian corals evolved to fill the niche they vacated during the Triassic, and still build reefs to this day. As the UK now sits too far north to develop its own Great Barrier Reef, we must look to these fossils to remind us of our more tropical past.

Parys Mountain

Staying on Anglesey but far from the east coast, to the north lies the island's best-known geological feature: Parys Mountain. A distinctly alien-looking world, the loose scree shows vibrant orange and red colours amongst the typical grey. Despite the name, this 'mountain' is nothing like what you find on the mainland. Instead of a conical peak there is a sudden fall to a deep pit, the exact opposite of what you expect from a traditional mountain.

The word 'lunar' is one often associated with the area, and fittingly it has been used as a filming location for several science-fiction works in the past. That 'distant alien planet' is actually only an hour's drive from Bangor.

There are no fossils here, but it is a site of great excavation. The sheer sides and distinct terracing in some areas tell the true history of this place. This is no natural formation, but instead the remains of a copper-mining operation, spanning many hundreds of years. There's evidence of mining activity here dating back to the Bronze Age, and 'cakes' of copper found bearing inscriptions of the Roman Empire. In the eighteenth century, Parys Mountain was the largest source of copper in Europe, so extensive that it gained the nickname of 'the copper kingdom'. During that time, the copper was largely used to clad naval ships, extending the lifespan and reliability of the ships by making it more difficult for encrusting creatures like barnacles to get a foothold. Much of the work was sadly sinister, being used for slave ships, the mine owner at the time being a strong supporter of the trade, who actively exchanged copper for human lives.

The geological history of the deposit is a much better story than the twisted legacy that humans imposed upon it. These mineral deposits date from the boundary of two geological periods, the Ordovician and the Silurian. Both of these periods were named after ancient Welsh tribes, the Ordovices and the Silures. When these rocks were being formed, Parys Mountain was part of a raging volcanic system.

Common rocks here are basalts and rhyolites, igneous indicators of the volcanic activity. The main copper veins lie immediately below these sudden interruptions of dark igneous rock in the later Ordovician. Along with the copper, the strata are also rich in deposits of zinc and iron.

Large deposits of metals in the ground have interesting effects on the habitat around it. The local plants evolve into specialist varieties, capable of surviving in metal-rich soils, and the water can show extreme pollution, especially when combined with mining activity (even when the mine itself hasn't been in operation for years). Visually, you can see this pollution in the form of the deep orange colour in the water. Such water discolouration is a common feature around mines, a trait made infamous by the enormous leeching of material around the Wheal Jane mine of Cornwall in 1992.

It's certainly worth noting that, in raw form, these materials can be very hazardous to humans, especially if ingested. I'm not implying you can eat the rocks, but geologists are known for their habit of licking and biting rocks as a method of identification (I am truly not joking here – licking and biting rocks is a legitimate technique employed by scientists). Given the risks, then, it is perhaps advisable not to indulge in that practice here. Unlike the places where shuffling through loose scree is encouraged, here at Parys Mountain it is wise to keep hands clear.

Snowdonia

Some of the most dramatic geological landscapes in Wales are to be found amongst the mountains of Snowdonia National Park, home of the country's tallest peaks. Mount Snowdon (Yr Wyddfa in Welsh) measures 1039 metres high from the lowest point, meaning that (by the mountaineering measure of prominence) it is the third-tallest mountain in the UK.

It's little wonder that much of Welsh mythology can trace its origins back to these weather-scarred valleys. This land was said to be the hunting grounds for the Annwn hounds, dogs of the underworld, and one peak is named after the seat of a giant: Cadair Idris.

Although rich in myth, the area is not overly populated with fossils, as most of the underlying geology of Snowdonia is igneous, remnants of that same volcanic system seen at Parys Mountain, which fell silent in the Ordovician. The mountains are dominated by ash-flow deposits and meta-morphic groups (those metamorphics including the iconic Welsh slates – source of all the best bakestones). However, there are some small sections of strata here to have survived unscathed. Surprisingly, one such area is around the pathway near the summit of Snowdon itself. Climbers can find shelly fragments of brachiopods and bivalves just about as far away from the sea floor as you can imagine getting in the UK, testament to the transformative power of the earth's tectonic forces. There are a few spots around the valleys where these dark shales (the Ffestiniog flagstones) crop up, with one of the regular finds there being the teardrop-shelled brachiopod *Lingulella*. These fossils date from the Cambrian, around half a billion years ago, and are some of the oldest fossils you can expect to discover in Britain, even if they are not particularly well preserved.

As with the Ordovician and Silurian seen on p.109, it is not a surprise to find Cambrian fossils in Wales, as this is yet another geological period named for the country. Cambrian is derived from the Latin name for Wales, 'Cambria' (that in turn originated from the Welsh, Cymru). Outside of geology, the word Cambrian is synonymous with Wales, adorning the titles of several regions of land and many pubs. These rocks around Snowdonia, first studied hundreds of years ago, inspired the naming of the age.

Mineral discoveries are more celebrated than fossil finds here, and none more so than Welsh gold. This has been mined and treasured by humans here for millennia, with hordes of golden jewellery having been discovered here, dating back some three thousand years ago.

The most productive of the gold mines was Clogau St David's, not far from the town of Bontddu in the south-west of Snowdonia. This mine has received some famous customers over the years, including multiple members of the British royal family, for whom Welsh gold is the material of choice for wedding rings.

After such a long life, the majority of Welsh gold mines closed in the late 1990s. Gold is a rare trace mineral in the earth and, with the efficiency of modern mining techniques, there is only so long you can collect it from a site before it goes beyond the point of economic feasibility. This doesn't mean there is no longer any gold there, but the major mineral deposits are nearly dry, and what is left would cost more to extract than would be made selling it. It is quite literally not worth its weight in gold.

Walking around nowadays, you would be exceptionally lucky to find any gold, but it isn't actually impossible, as small samples survive in stream beds around the old mines. Temper expectations, though; you aren't going to be finding stray nuggets like those that inspired the gold rushes of the American West. Any gold here will be in the form of tiny individual flecks, glinting within the darker rock matrix; almost invisible unless you have a trained eye and know exactly what to look for.

The rich geology of Snowdon extends underground with a multitude of cave systems, some natural, some man-made. In them, you can find a rich spectrum of natural and human history, from the copper mines of Cygun to incredible modern uses, like the slate caves of Blaenau, which have been transformed into an underground trampoline park. Wales as a whole has bountiful caves, none more famous or beautiful than the Dan yr Ogof National Showcaves much further south in the Brecon Beacons.

Once again, like the highlands of Scotland or interior Northern Ireland, Snowdonia suffers partially from a lack of fossil-hunting locations due to its dynamic geological past. But it is that same geology that gives the area endless awe-inspiring natural scenes.

Upper Gilwern

Those three geological periods mentioned in the last two sections that take their names from Welsh history (the Cambrian, the Ordovician and the Silurian) are the first three of the Phanerozoic eon, the first division of time to contain complex life, dating back more than half a billion years ago right up to today. Being early on in this eon makes them a spectacularly important time in life history, when some of the first major animal diversification events were taking place. These periods dominate most of north and mid-Wales's geology and preserve some of the icons of the ancient world, creatures we've encountered in a few sites already, the trilobites.

The shape of a trilobite is one familiar in pop-cultural depictions of palaeontology, a classic fossil shape, somewhat reminiscent in appearance of a living woodlouse. At the front of the animal is a large, usually semi-circular mass, followed up by a series of repeating body segments, before tapering off at the end, giving the animal an oval shape.

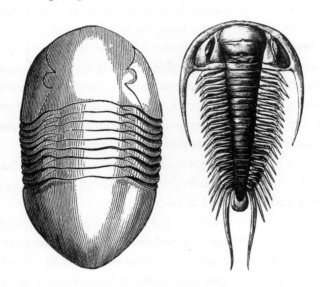

Two distinct trilobite morphs, different but both showing
the three-lobed structure

That rounded section at the front is the head, which scientists refer to as the cephalon. Each body segment that follows would have served as protection for a pair of legs housed underneath, which would have been used for scurrying along the sea floor (or in some cases swimming). We know they lived underwater, both thanks to their modes of preservation, but also due to the best specimens showing gills on their undersides too, with a pair of gills accompanying each pair of legs.

The final few sections of the body were fused together into a rudimentary kind of tail, which science gives the name pygidium. This divides the trilobite into three main sections: the cephalon (head), thorax (middle), and the pygidium (tail). This segmentation makes the name trilobite (literally meaning 'three lobes') seem all the more fitting.

Most animals are hard-wired by evolution to recognise faces quickly, and as such you'll immediately spot a key feature on the head of a trilobite. They had eyes. Although not notable now, this was a huge evolutionary leap for the time. Trilobites possessed some of the first complex eyes of any animal, ever. It is thought that prior to this, there only existed very simple eyes, capable of detecting light and dark without much precision. But the evolution of the complex eye opened up a new world of possibilities.

Exploiting this new sense led to more sophisticated predators that were better able to hunt down prey, sparking an eternal evolutionary arms race. Because of this, animals like trilobites evolved their exoskeletons for protection. These skeletons are far more likely to preserve as fossils, and so, when reading the rock record, you see an enormous increase in fossils at around this point in time. In palaeontology, we refer to this event as the Cambrian explosion. Although the exact timing is debated, this incredible diversification is without doubt one of the most important events in the history of the planet.

There are a number of places with potential to find trilobites, but I'm going to highlight what is probably the best in Wales, Upper Gilwern Quarry in Powys. By the time these trilobites entered the picture, it was many millions of years past the Cambrian Explosion. The Upper Gilwern specimens are from a little under 470 million years ago, in the Ordovician. They are preserved here as compressed flat fossils in dark shales, easily split open with a decent hammer blow. This site in particular is renowned for yielding complete specimens, although due to the nature of their bodies, you will frequently find them fragmented. Thanks to their splaying segments giving them a passing resemblance to the flying insects, the isolated pygidiums of some species are known as 'stone butterflies' in Welsh folklore, likely connected to Arthurian legend.

The most common trilobite of Gilwern is *Ogyginus*, a classically shaped trilobite with quite a sizeable pygidium. It also has cephalic spines, a feature you see in several trilobite species wherein their head shield has elongated 'fingers' extending on either side. These are quite small in *Ogyginus*, but in other species they can be extremely long, like the Moroccan *Cyphaspides*, in which they can extend beyond the length of the body.

The famous Upper Gilwern Quarry is on private land, but it is accessible with permission from the landowner. As always with such sites, remember to do your own up-to-date research before setting out to make sure access rights haven't changed. There are other sites around where trilobites can be found, but it involves a lot more prospecting, and that's not an appealing idea unless you fancy getting lost in rural Wales. I hope you can read the road signs.

South and West Wales

Penarth and Lavernock

My opinion that the south of Wales is one of the best places on earth could be viewed as being somewhat biased, given that I grew up there. However, it is without any bias that I can say that one of the best places to find fossils in all of Wales is in the south, at the beaches of Penarth and Lavernock, the stretch of coast next to Cardiff.

So close are these sites to the capital that the cliffs of Penarth are clearly visible across the waters of Cardiff Bay. They're predominantly red in colour, with bands of blue-grey and yellow limestone, and thin layers of mudstone. The fossiliferous grey rocks are packed with fossils from the end of the Triassic and early Jurassic age (around 200 million years ago), preserving marine life around this first major Mesozoic transition, the end of the Triassic period being marked by an extinction event across the planet, driven by climate change.

Penarth has long been a resort town, as evidenced by the beautiful Victorian pier. The pier can be used as a dividing line, with some fossils far more abundant on one side than the other, reflecting a rising sea level across this time (seen in the rocks from east to west). Amongst the most common fossils to the left side of the pier (when facing the water) are the smooth, rounded shells of the bivalves *Plagiostoma*. Larger than the typical bivalves found in most UK fossil locations, these often reach a size that is roughly equivalent to the palm of your hand. In the local palaeontological world, this size and quality has earned them the appreciative nickname of 'Juicy Bives', a name that has even been used at conferences as a term of endearment for a group of organisms that all too often go unloved.

At their best, these *Plagiostoma* can be found complete, with both valves whole and still joined. With the grey rock matrix removed, you could believe them to have been recently fished out from the water. Their shell rigidity doesn't cope too well with temperature or humidity fluctuations, so once exposed (if not kept in the right environment), they may fragment. This means that for every perfectly preserved shell you find, you're likely to see several where the shells have fractured into squared sections in the rock, as though exploding in slow motion.

The cliffs on this side of the pier are exceptionally tall, and extra care needs to be taken near them as they're eroding fast, much to the misfortune of the houses on the clifftops. You can find plenty in the rocks on the shore, however, with marine invertebrates, including ammonites, quite common.

On the right side of the pier stretches a long sea wall, before once more reaching cliff exposures towards Lavernock Point. Speaking from personal experience, it could be said that the tall cliffs to the left of the pier are where the fossils are frequent but less spectacular, whereas to the right, fossil finds are rarer but often more memorable. Here, vertebrate remains can be found more frequently. Bones in the grey limestone regularly appear as brown or black in colour, with ichthyosaurs being the most common finds. This is the best place in Wales to find the remains of these sea monsters.

One of the most extraordinary finds in this area occurred in 2014, by fossil-hunting brothers Rob and Nick Hanigan. A cliff fall nearby revealed material from the earliest Jurassic period (201 million years ago), and the pair came across a jumble of bones belonging to a new species of animal. Of all the fragments, one piece in particular caught the eye, the tip of a small snout bearing an unmistakably distinctive tooth.

This feature, combined with claws and other skeletal elements, confirmed that what they'd discovered were the remains of a carnivorous dinosaur. This was the first Welsh representative of the group known as theropods. Christened with a name fitting for an ancient Welsh 'dragon', it was dubbed *Dracoraptor*.

The theropods are an umbrella group for the meat-eating dinosaurs, containing some of the biggest names in palaeontology, such as the celebrity *Tyrannosaurus* and *Velociraptor*, those misfit Cretaceous stars of the Jurassic Park franchise. The media naturally jumped on this connection straight away and flooded the scientific news with reports of 'the Welsh *T. rex*'.

This is, in fact, rather inaccurate, as being in the same extended evolutionary family doesn't necessarily make the pair close: *Dracoraptor* is quite an early dinosaur, and, at the time of writing, it remains the oldest dinosaur discovery within the Jurassic period, around 130 million years older than *T. rex* (which was so late in the Mesozoic as to have the misfortune of being able to physically witness the asteroid strike that doomed them). As such, *Dracoraptor* is nestled much nearer the base of the family tree, closer to nippy beasts like *Ceolophysis* and *Eoraptor*.

This is reflected in the dinosaur's size and build as well. *Dracoraptor* is far from the giant killer we know as *T rex*. (which grew to about twelve metres in length), with an adult *Dracoraptor* only measuring up to three metres in length and standing about one metre off the ground. Lightly built and fairly agile-looking, this predator would have focused on much smaller prey.

Enough of the dinosaur was discovered that a reconstruction was able to be built. Made by palaeo-artist Bob Nicholls, it now stands in the National Museum of Wales in Cardiff. The first thing you notice upon seeing the model is that it has been given a plumage of bright orange feathers. There is no direct evidence in the fossils of *Dracoraptor* having feathers, but scientifically, it is actually a very reasonable theory.

The fact that dinosaurs are the ancestors of modern birds isn't really news any more; this accepted theory of familial connection has been around for long enough to have entered mainstream science knowledge. But just how closely they are related, and the prevalence of uniquely 'bird' features they possessed, is often still surprising. Recent research suggests that feathers first appeared millions of years earlier than we initially believed, towards the very base of the dinosaur family tree. This idea could even propose the strange thought that, for many dinosaurs, feathers were actually the 'default'; that is, that they began with feathers and those dinosaurs that we know did have scales would have had to evolve in order to lose their feathers and return to typical reptilian scales.

Even the colouration of the model isn't a complete stab in the dark but is instead grounded in real science. Fossil feathers and skin can preserve the remains of microscopic pigment structures, and these can indicate the potential colour of the animal. Research into feathers of a small predatory dinosaur from China, *Sinosauropteryx*, revealed its colour in life as ginger and white, like that displayed on the *Dracoraptor* model. Much of this modern research is fascinating, but there are plenty of other works on this topic out there, should you wish to explore it in more depth.

Penarth is a great starter location for fossil hunting, thanks to the abundance of finds and the amenities readily available on site, with plenty of parking and transport options. Lavernock is a little bit further out of the way, but transport is still relatively simple. Failing that, the walk is doable from the pier in only forty minutes.

An important caveat, though: you should never attempt to make such a journey unless you've consulted the tide times. This site needs extra mention of this because, although awareness of the tide is always important, it is nowhere more so than here. The small town of Penarth is home to not only the largest tidal range in the UK, but one of the very largest in the world – up to a staggering 14-metre difference. It is not uncommon to see the end of the pier bone dry as the waters recede, only for the sea to flood the coastal road a few hours later. Beyond fossils, the changing tide here is an extraordinary thing to behold in and of itself.

Barry Island

Following the coast from Lavernock, you'll reach the resort town of Barry. For the past century or more, Barry Island has been well known as a seaside attraction; the sandy beach and amusement park draw in people from all over, in spite of the misnomer, as Barry Island isn't actually an island at all.

There is some interesting rock on show here, with the large spit of land known as Friar's Point extending from the west side of the beach. Fossils within this rock are predominantly Carboniferous corals that erode out of the limestone, as well as connections of tightly packed crinoid ossicles. Though interesting, these aren't as impressive as what you can find if you backtrack down the coast a bit, beyond the docks to a section called the Bendricks.

Bendrick Rock is considered such an important site in UK geology that it's actually listed for protection twice: once for geological sequences, and once for the trace fossils that lure in the palaeontologists.

The flat beds of the foreshore are Triassic sandstones, about 220 million years old and bearing that distinctive red colouration often associated with rocks of this age. The thin horizontal beds continue up the small cliffs and form a uniquely complete geological sequence, but when it comes to fossils, it is necessary to look underfoot. We're back onto those most beloved of all trace fossils: dinosaur footprints.

At about fifteen centimetres in length, the Bendricks trackways reveal the classic three-toed dinosaur shape. Though the *Dracoraptor* may have been the first theropod officially discovered in Wales, it has long been known that they must have been here, as these footprints are almost certainly from one of their relatives. Like the Storeton Woods specimen (see p.89), the specific species is not known, but the tracks have been given a scientific name, in this case *Anchisauripus*.

The Bendricks also give a lesson in looking after local discoveries, as they have twice been the victims of criminal damage. In 2012, some of the prints were removed by vandals and thankfully later recovered, and another attempt was made to rip some out in 2014. Since then, some have been preserved in the National Museum of Wales, and others remain on the beach for all to see and study.

The amateur removal of such fossils is reckless and selfish, and certainly not the kind of thing to be attempted on a personal whim. It will almost certainly cause irreversible damage to an irreplaceable fossil, and lead to an individual being charged for criminal damage. Areas like this are protected for a reason, and when left in peace they can be enjoyed by all.

Beyond the Bendricks also lies another point of interest to demonstrate the enormous difference the tide can make on the borders of the Bristol Channel. Like at Barry, Sully Island is partially a misleading name, as, depending on when you visit, you may or may not find an island at all. A thin isthmus (strip of land) walkway stretches out to the exposed mass of red rock, topped by coastal grasses.

The rock here is also Triassic and acts to preserve what would have been a lagoonal shore in the midst of a vast Pangaean desert (all the earth's continents being joined into one enormous landmass at this time). There isn't much in the way of fossils here, though there's plenty of opportunity for the discovery of rabbits, which have long been the rulers of the island.

Anyone who walks here must watch the tide carefully as it comes in quickly and locks off the island twice a day. Those on the island when the waters return will be stuck there for several hours. Thankfully, signs at the site clearly state the times at which it is and isn't safe to cross.

There are several places where this same process happens, such as the famous St Michael's Mount in Cornwall, but I've included Sully here purely to re-emphasise the power of the tide at the Bristol Channel, and why extra care should be taken whenever fossil hunting on any coastline. After seeing the incredible effect water has on solid rock cliffs, you'd do well to pay it due respect.

Southerndown

Just south of Bridgend are the cliffs of Southerndown and Dunraven Bay. Somewhat imposing with their sheer walls and regular striations of shale and limestone, the beaches in front of the cliffs may seem familiar, even to new visitors, as this location is so often used for filming by the BBC. A vast amount of time is covered by these cliffs, from the early Carboniferous to the Jurassic Blue Lias. The fossils originate from these later stages and, whilst many layers can seem barren and impenetrable at first, the cliffs can quite literally rain fossils down onto the beach.

Regularly scattered around the rocks on the northern shore are countless examples of one very distinctive fossil, a curved grey shell striped with multiple clear growth bands. These creatures resemble contorted oysters, which they are, perhaps unsurprisingly, related to. Their shape has earned them the slightly grotesque nickname of 'devil's toenails' but, to science, and those who could do without such images, they're called *Gryphaea*.

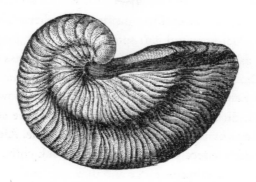

A classic *Gryphaea* or 'Devil's Toenail' fossil

Gryphaea are exceptionally common fossils, seemingly omnipresent across so many UK fossil-hunting sites. The only reason they aren't as ubiquitous with palaeontology as ammonites is due to our inherent preference towards more aesthetically pleasing intricate spirals as opposed to fossils resembling grey toenail clippings.

The reason these fossils are worth noting here in particular, rather than any of the other previous locations they can be found, is simply that there are few locations where *Gryphaea* are as numerous as they are here at Southerndown. So common are they that, on one of my recent trips there, I challenged myself to see how many I could find without moving my feet. Firmly rooted to the ground, I tossed over the pebbles within reach and picked up every *Gryphaea* revealed. At the point when my cradled arms were literally overflowing with them, I figured I'd proven my point.

Being bivalves, their shells are made of two parts. The 'toenail' section is one of these, whilst the other lays flat and thin at the wide end of the curve, acting like a lid to keep safe the soft body of the mollusc inside. It is believed that these creatures would have sat lid-up on the sea floor, filtering out plankton from the current. A word used to describe this kind of lifestyle in animals is to say that they're 'recliners'.

Gryphaea were a long-lived group; first appearing towards the end of the Triassic, they survived and flourished throughout the dinosaur age. Often found together, it's believed they probably lived in groups, forming mass assemblages on the sea floor. This large temporal range and their sturdy, shelled bodies contributes to their abundance in the fossil record today.

There are thirty-eight recognised species of *Gryphaea*, usually identified by the 'teeth' structures around the hinge of the two valves. This feature is regularly hidden or else has not been preserved well enough to be examined closely, making on-the-spot identifications difficult without consulting a specialist. The most common species to be found is G. *arcuata*, so odds are that if you're in a locality with that blue-hued limestone of the Jurassic Lias, this is the species you're collecting.

But there are more than bivalves in these cliffs. The usual suspects of the Blue Lias are all here in the limestone: ammonites, marine reptiles and fish, falling in boulders from the cliffs above. Traces of corals can also be discovered in the more ancient rocks. The most impressive finds are predominantly from the southern end of the bay, though they are much rarer. They may well be hidden in nodules but can be exposed with a decent hammer blow.

Extensive sections of fossilised wood can also be found here, remains of the *Araucaria* conifer trees that made up Jurassic forests, the wood having ended up in the sea after the tree had fallen (possibly due to flash flooding). Wood is quite easy to misinterpret as weathered bone, as both of them regularly preserve as black against the grey rock. However, the structure of the two is quite different. Bone preserves with a honeycomb-like texture, whereas wood is flakier, and you may even be able to see some more familiar bark structures in the fossilised wood to be found here.

Glamorgan Quarries

As we've already seen from the Permian fish of Durham (see p.76), there are still places in the UK where active quarries play key roles in palaeontological discoveries. Being private, commercially run operations, these aren't usually accessible to the public, but their influence on the story of British prehistory makes them well worth mentioning. Hence why it is worth highlighting the discoveries made at several quarries in the Vale of Glamorgan.

By the late Triassic, this area of Britain was an archipelago; islands dotted around a shallow sea in tropical conditions, as different as it is possible to imagine from the modern Wales we know today. Exposed to the water, the soluble limestone cliffs were eroded to form extensive cave systems along the coast.

Caves, then, as now, act as collecting points for the remains of animals and just about anything else that happened to wash into the sea. Preserved in the sediment here is a literal mash-up of all kinds of remains, often smashed apart and jumbled together by the violent actions of the waves that brought them here. The result is what's known as a 'fissure fill' system, where pockets of younger rock are found within much older strata. In this case, little windows into the Triassic are found in rock that is otherwise from the Carboniferous.

These fissure fills are common around the Bristol Channel, where limestone and aggregate has been mined for construction for generations. Over the lifespan of these mines, some have revealed hidden secrets from the Triassic deposits, fossils of the animals unlucky enough to be washed in.

The best-known discovery (and a personal favourite) was picked up by Walter Kuhne in Duchy Quarry in 1949, a find that could so easily have been missed, serving to prove that not all the most interesting fossils of the Mesozoic were from giant reptiles, and that it's worth having a look at the finer sediments we ignore all too often.

What Kuhne discovered was a single, and absolutely minute, molar tooth in the rock. Fortunately, a tooth is often just about the most indicative feature of an animal you can find, and as such, it revealed one key fact about this creature: it was a mammal.

Mammal finds this ancient are rare and, living around 205 million years ago, this is still the oldest mammal species yet discovered in the UK. Such an important find was named proudly after the area, dubbing it *Morganucodon*, translating to 'Glamorgan tooth'. Many in the palaeontological community know this little one by a more affectionate pet name: Morgie.

Over the following decade, further excavations served to reveal a much fuller picture of Morgie. The entire skull measured only three centimetres in length, with the whole animal's body being about the same size as a common mole. Like most early mammals, *Morganucodon* was an insectivore and likely nocturnal, relying on the cover of night to avoid the dinosaurs, who were well on their way to global domination. Though the dinosaurs may have evolved around the same time as mammals, it was dinosaurs who first staked their claim to the planet.

Usually, mammals are defined by characteristics such as fur and mammary glands, things which aren't preserved here (though we assume Morgie did have fur). With this one, the most interesting elements lay in the teeth and jaws. The teeth are a distinctive mammalian shape, and the lower jaw comprised of only one bone, the dentary. This is something we don't often think about but is in fact a very mammalian trait. In reptiles, like dinosaurs, their lower jaw is made of three separate bones. There is even evidence that Morgie may have possessed a system of tooth replacement similar to ours (with a set of 'baby' and then 'adult' teeth).

Morganucodon was far from the only small animal of the time to avoid the limelight due to the more famous residents, with other fragmentary fossils unveiling an entire community at the feet of the dinosaurs. Recent research has placed focus on a group of reptiles called clevosaurs, discovered in the Pant-y-Ffynnon quarry (between Cardiff and Bridgend).

Clevosaurs belong to an order of animals that today have only one living descendent, the Tuatara of New Zealand. Though they do look very much like lizards, they are in fact their own distinct group, with an ancient lineage dating to the Triassic. This timing is why Tuataras are so regularly falsely advertised as 'living dinosaurs', despite not being particularly closely related to them.

Like Morgie, clevosaurs are small and studied mostly from their teeth. This work is ongoing, with a new species having been announced from this quarry as recently as 2018, when *Clevosaurus cambrica* was first described by palaeontologists Emily Keeble and Dr David Whiteside.

To further expand on the point of these living right under the feet of dinosaurs, thirty years previously, in that same Pant-y-Ffynnon quarry, a dinosaur was found. For about twenty years, this dinosaur was thought to be a species already known from Bristol, England, but, in 2007, it was recognised as actually being unique. This gave it the distinction of being the very first new dinosaur species found in Wales. However, recent research has proposed a potential reversal of this decision.

Studies of the re-christened and (at time of writing still valid name) *Pantydraco* revealed more about this early dinosaur. As with most Triassic dinosaurs living on an island system with such limited resources, *Pantydraco* had yet to achieve the kind of huge sizes its relatives would later be known for. This two-legged animal would have grown to about three metres in length, and preserves an intriguing time in their evolution.

The very first dinosaurs are thought to have been carnivorous (like *Dracoraptor*, seen on p.119), but we know that eventually there would come to be a massive diversity of herbivorous species as well. *Pantydraco* might well record a step in that transition, as some dinosaurs began to adapt to the vegetarian diet, evolving to fill every niche the ecosystem had to offer. Studies on its teeth suggest it to have been an omnivore, eating both plants and meat. Many millions of years later, the relatives of this small Welsh dinosaur would fully commit to the herbivorous diet and go on to be the most relentless plant-processing machines the earth has ever seen, the gigantic sauropods (some of which could grow to over twenty metres in length).

Scientists continue to make discoveries in these quarries, including a new species of theropod dinosaur in 2021. The small coelophysoid was named *Pendraig milnerae*, both for its Welsh location and in honour of famed NHM palaeontologist, Angela Milner.

Though these quarries are currently still in use and out of reach, as with all mining operations, there will come a day when they're no longer economically viable and will shut down. The mines, and potentially fossil-rich spoil heaps, could then well be opened to the public. We can't say for certain that this will happen or when, but many of the locations in this book began as inaccessible quarries, so there is hope that, in the future, more amazing discoveries will be made here by amateur hunters.

St David's

Extending westwards from South Wales towards Ireland can be found what is, by population, the smallest city in the UK: St David's. Surrounding the city of fewer than two thousand people is the rugged Pembrokeshire coastline, one of the most picturesque landscapes in the country. Subjected to some of the harshest conditions in Wales, with wild weather and exposure to the sea, this land has been carved into many bays and inlets, creating prime fossil-collecting opportunities.

Most of the fossils around here can be dated to the Palaeozoic, that expansive era before the dinosaur age (stretching from around 540 to 250 million years ago), and there are rare occurrences where the fossils are possibly even older than this. Very near to the city is Whitesands Bay, a popular destination for tourists in the summer due to the smooth quartz-sand beaches, but flanking the open sands are rocky escarpments containing fossils.

Facing the water and heading right, you will come across thin beds of grey silt and mudstones, jutting directly out from the water when the tide is in. Fossils in these rocks are rare, usually no more than fragments of brachiopod shells entombed in the bedrock. It is sad to say that the best of fossils here are ones you might otherwise look straight past in more bountiful areas.

What makes the fossils of this bay so significant, however, is that they're from the Cambrian period, like those seen in Snowdonia (see p.110). They may not be numerous or particularly glamorous, but at about 506 million years old, they're the oldest fossils you will find in South Wales and some of the oldest you're likely to come across in the whole of the UK.

For better odds of making interesting finds, the best location of the St David's area is to the north. Here lies Abereiddy Bay, probably the best-regarded fossil site in Pembrokeshire. The beach here is not the same bright quartz you see at Whitesands, but instead a darker, grittier sediment and shingle. Abereiddy is all about the rocks, and the tourists who come to the water's edge here are more commonly hunting for fossils than the summer sun.

The rocky outcrops on the south end of the bay are dark shales, which regularly flake off after rough weather and are subsequently scattered along the shore. This makes hunting for fossils relatively simple, scouring the shingle for the black shales and looking for the streaks of white from the fossils. By far the most common find at Abereiddy are bizarre creatures we've seen before in Scotland, graptolites, the floating filter feeders with some similarity to corals (see p.41).

Many consider Abereiddy Bay to be the single best location in the UK to find these saw-like sea creatures. The species here act as zone fossils, providing an excellent way to date the strata. One of the more abundant species is *Didymograptus murchisoni*. This dates the strata to about 463 million years old, making the fossils around 13 million years older than the Scottish graptolites, but still within that same geological period called the Ordovician.

When we last encountered graptolites on p.42, it was mentioned that they came in a variety of different body shapes, and those of Pembrokeshire are remarkably different from those up north. The species we saw previously (*Orthograptus*) had a single stipe with theca coming off either side, giving it the double-edged saw-blade look. However, *Didymograptus* is a pendant shape: it has two stipes forming a tight 'U', like a tuning fork. The theca face inwards, running along the inside line of the pendant, with the outer edge smooth.

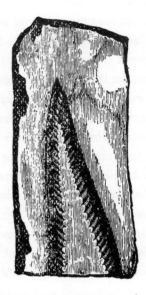

Didymograptus, showing its pendant shape

These are just two of the forms graptolites can take. Else-where, there are species that are the reverse of this shape, some where the stipes stretch out horizontally, and some with more than two stipes. In life, it is thought that these creatures may have had soft-body flotation aids above them to keep them suspended in the water column. It's hard to put an accurate reconstruction of graptolites together, as there are truly no animals like them alive today. But you won't be short of their fossils at Abereiddy Bay, lying exposed in the rock fragments or easily revealed by splitting loose shales.

As well as the fossils, the continued beauty of Pembroke-shire can't be ignored, especially here, so close to Wales's own

Blue Lagoon. This name is frequently given to distinct areas of vibrantly coloured and scenic pools of water the world over. Here in Wales, it is the enclosed nature of the bay, calmer than the waters beyond, and the striking contrast of the marine colours with the black shale that make it stand out.

This lagoon is not an entirely natural feature, though, instead being a relic of a former slate mine, the ruins of which can still be seen on site. Protruding from the northern arm of the bay, the 'Slate Quarryman's Cottage' is slowly being weathered away, much like the strata around it.

Having been abandoned over a hundred years ago, the quarry now has a second life as a tourist destination after inadvertently becoming a site of 'natural' beauty. The 25-metre deep waters have played host to many adventurous travellers over the years, even once hosting a global competition for cliff diving.

Both Abereiddy and Whitesands are easy to access, being relatively popular sites to visit near St David's, both offering room to park and good degrees of accessibility, with paths going directly to the shore. Pembrokeshire has more to offer than just these two localities, however, and more lie following the coastline to the south, towards the westernmost point of Wales.

South Pembrokeshire

The Pembrokeshire coast follows an inverted 'C' shape around St Brides Bay, famed as a sanctuary for wildlife, with thriving communities of dolphins and other marine creatures. So far, we've looked at the northern side of this large National Park, but now we turn our attention across the water to the other ends of this impressive expanse of wild Wales.

Tracing around the edge of St Brides Bay are exposures such as Druidstone Haven, where the strata and fossils may seem quite familiar; the same black rocks with white grapto-lites seen up the coast at Abereiddy. As we've covered these animals twice already (see p.40 and 134), we won't go into detail other than to say they are a few million years younger than the Abereiddy specimens, and are represented by single stiped forms like those seen in Scotland.

It is the living residents of the coast that most commonly attract visitors to the headland at the far end of St Brides Bay. The islands of Skomer and Skokholm are treasured for their seabird colonies, with thousands of breeding puffins utilising the islands' safety from mainland predators to nest. The puffins have become a beloved symbol of this part of the country.

Directly across the water from Skokholm is a flat stretch of open shore, Marloes Sands. This is another one of Wales's popular seaside resort locations, with many people coming down to this part of the UK in the summer. Any visitor here will also be taken with the striking geology.

The progression of strata here is dramatic; the beds of rock are standing on their ends, reaching towards the sky, having been turned to be almost perpendicular to the modern beach. This incredible vertical banding of the rock continues beyond the cliffs, as small islands of rock stand marooned in the sand and mudflats.

There are fossils here (mostly seashell fragments), but before that, another geological feature can't help but catch your eye – the ripple beds. These structures were never alive but do capture a snapshot of the environment at the time. If proof were ever needed that these towering walls of stone were once horizontal and underwater, then there can be no doubt when looking at the surface of the ripple beds. Ripple marks are a commonly preserved feature in sedimentary rocks, preserving the actions of the ancient waves that once undulated the sand. Their formation is relatively straightforward, and you can see it in action today. All you need to do is go to the water's edge and see them exposed as the tide retreats.

We can learn a lot from ripples, recording details about ancient environments that really let us breathe details into our picture of the lost worlds. For example, their symmetry tells us which direction the water flowed. Symmetrical ripples indicate a steady tide, regularly coming in and retreating out, whilst asymmetrical ripples can point to a dominant flow direction. If, when looking at a ripple, you can see a shallow and gradual rise from left to right, followed by a sudden drop off, and then repeated, then the water was also flowing from left to right.

Ripples aren't always formed by water action; they can be generated by the wind as well. In vast deserts, wind action can create vast dune systems which also record in the strata. There's a whole world of sedimentary structures within the rocks that can tell us about the past environment. We don't have the time to get into them all here, but the amazing world of sedimentology holds many tricks for reconstructing the past in much greater detail than one might at first think.

Though they're common in the rock record, it's not often you find expanses of ripples as intact as those at Marloes

Sands. The surfaces of some cliff faces are covered entirely in them, the ghosts of a tidal system which ceased to be in the Silurian, and yet they appear fresh enough that you could believe the modern sea had only just uncovered them (that is, if not for the notable fact they're in absolutely the wrong orientation, owing to the fact that the ancient sea that formed them is long gone).

Most of the time when ripples are discovered, they are either hidden away within the rock or smashed up into little fragments strewn across the shore, as happens to all cliff rocks, so it's a treat to see them grouped together as they are here.

Shelly invertebrate fossils such as brachiopods are the most common fossils you're likely to pick up from here, also dating to the Silurian. They aren't the most spectacular fossils, but they are interesting as it's quite common to find them looking a little bit strange.

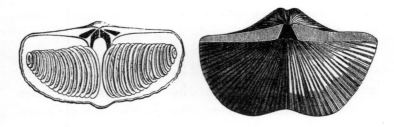

Brachiopods with a 'winged' shell

Certain layers of the rock have felt the strain of the tectonic activity more than others, and some of the most productive fossil beds of Marloes Sands are also the ones to have been most deformed by the uplifting and folding of the earth. This has in some cases warped the shapes of the fossils to be oddly shaped out, going from circular to more elliptical. Several structures within the rock caused by the immense shearing stresses are also strongly visible here.

Sedimentary and structural features are a huge topic in themselves, and one with their own mark printed on rocks all over the world the same as fossils, making it impossible to cover them in the same space. But they can be fascinating, and here in the cliffs of Cymru are some of the best places in the UK to see them.

West Midlands

Wren's Nest

Fossil locations are so often synonymous with the coastline of Britain that, when people consider which regions may be best for prospecting, the Midlands are regularly overlooked. To do this would be a mistake, though, as some of the richest sites in the country are to be found here.

Almost as if to prove this fact, there is one such excellent site in surprisingly close proximity to the second-largest city in the UK, one of the last places you might expect to find fossil exposures. The town of Dudley, just ten miles from the centre of Birmingham, is home to the Wren's Nest nature reserve, an oasis of natural history amongst the urbanised landscape. Such is the importance of this site that in 1956 it was proclaimed a National Nature Reserve, quite unlike any other reserve before it. Wren's Nest was not selected for preservation due to the local fauna and flora, or at least, not the living examples. This was the first area in the UK protected exclusively on the basis of its unique geology. The most famous resident of the site, plastered on signs across the town and even prominently featuring on the borough's coat of arms is the 'Dudley Bug'.

Even if you've never heard of the bug before, there's no mistaking that shape. One of the most recognisable in the fossil world, it's clearly a trilobite. We've spoken of them before on p. 114, but it's worth revisiting such an important group.

The Dudley Bug is a member of the species *Calymene blumenbachii*, first discovered at the Wren's Nest and cropping up in scientific publications as early as 1752, decades before geology would start to make sense of what exactly had been found. Some of the first theories postulated that it was a large locust, which would make it the most bizarrely proportioned locust known to science (though you can still find signs that refer to it as the Dudley Locust).

A *Calymene* trilobite, aka the Dudley Bug

Some of these theories may seem laughable to palaeontologists today, but we must put ourselves in the mindsets of the people of the time, with absolutely no frame of reference for comparison. The best analogy, and one that still serves well as a visual description today, is that trilobites appear to be rather like woodlice. It's a comparison that is apt in some ways, but not all. Unlike woodlice, trilobites lived underwater, were not crustaceans, and had many more legs than woodlice

(woodlice have fourteen, whilst trilobites could have as many as forty). Later discoveries would reveal that both groups are able to curl up into balls for defence, however.

A big difference between the trilobites here and those of Upper Gilwern (see p.113) is that at Wren's Nest you're more likely to find them preserved with a three-dimensional structure as a result of their early cementation making them more resistant to the compression of the overlying rock. This reveals a few more features, such as the bulbous structure in the middle-front of their heads. This is not a braincase, as you might presume; instead, this is where the animal stored its stomach.

Another thing this three-dimensional structure can highlight are the eyes, which offers up more information than just their evolutionary importance. Like an insect, trilobite eyes are compound, made up of a collection of individual lenses. But, unlike insects, these lenses were composed of crystalline calcite. Their eyes were made of rock, even before they fossilised.

A classic example of a trilobite, clearly showing the three lobes

The *Calymene* trilobites are younger than those seen previously, with the rocks of Wren's Nest dating to the Silurian, 430 million years ago. As evidenced by their repeated appearances in the fossil record, the trilobites were a successful and long-lived group, existing on earth for around 290 million years before they became perhaps the highest-profile victims of the Permian mass extinction, the major climate change event that wiped out around 96 per cent of marine life about 250 million years ago. To squash another popular fallacy, this does mean that trilobites had already been extinct for several million years by the time dinosaurs first evolved.

All the common names of Silurian marine fossils can be found here too, with brachiopods, bivalves, corals, bryozoans and crinoids to name a few. The fairly regular falling of rocks from the large exposures of Wren's Nest keeps new material appearing.

Proud of its palaeontological heritage, this surrounding area of Dudley boasts of its collections, with places like the charmingly named 'Fossil View Road'. This location also features what some palaeontologists deem to be the holy grail of fossil-hunting localities, having a pub so close that it's basically on site. It's a recurring joke among palaeontologists that if you check the scientific literature, you'll find a study bias that correlates quite nicely with those sites with the best proximity to a local watering hole.

Wren's Nest is easy to find and travel to, and a site that is well looked after by the local community. It's one of several places in this book where guided tours are available, perfect for those just getting started in the fossil world who want to know more of the area's history and be shown the best places to scour for the rocky treasures.

Being such a protected site, in addition to all the rules which apply to SSSIs, there are absolutely no hammers permitted in the Wren's Nest location without special permission. Any fossils collected here must be taken from the loose scree that tumbles from the strata. On a good day, though, this area can be so bountiful in fossils that you won't be impeded by any restrictions.

Wenlock Edge

Wren's Nest isn't the only place in the West Midlands where one can find Silurian treasures. This region is particularly rich in these fossils thanks to one specific geological unit, the Wenlock Series, named after the Shropshire town of Much Wenlock. One of the best places to find these fossils is on the National Trust land that borders the western side of the town, Wenlock Edge, next to the Shropshire Hills.

The fossils of Wenlock are known throughout the world due to their exceptional quality, having been buried rapidly in fine sediment, thus preserving much greater detail. It is common to hear them referenced as a benchmark of excellence for comparison. This is another one of the sites given the title of *Lagerstätte* (scientific term used for an area of exceptional preservation), like the collections seen at Rhynie (see p.29). The Wenlock series shows a stunningly diverse reef system dating back around 430 million years, hugely abundant in marine invertebrates, including brachiopods, trilobites, crinoids, corals and more, preserved in three dimensions and with the finest details of their shells visible.

The strata are predominantly tough nodular limestones, not particularly easy to split open and likely to cause damage to the fossils inside if attempted. When it comes to Wenlock stone, it's best to take the advice of the Wren's Nest site seen on p.144, leaving the hammer out of it and doing more careful preparation later, such as slowly removing the matrix with an air abrasive.

What the Wenlock series truly serves to highlight is just how different the reefs of the past were compared to those we think of today. In our modern oceans we are used to a plethora of colourful fish species swimming around the corals, but in the Silurian, about 428 million years ago, the fish we are used to (which mostly belong to a group called teleosts) were millions of years away from evolving. The Wenlock series shows us a world where the dominant reef fauna were invertebrates.

Stromatoporoids (calcified sponges) and rugose and tabulate corals build much of the reef, with crinoids also particularly dominant. Though it is still difficult to find these sea lilies intact, you can find whole sections of stalk where the ossicles are held together. If you find these, they can sometimes look almost like oddly bendy constructions of rebar.

Brachiopods and bivalves can accumulate in huge numbers, forming layers that can make it appear that the regular patches of limestone are the oddity in the shell-fossil matrix. The high-quality preservation can also preserve another difference between these two visually similar organisms. In bivalves, the apex of the shell tapers to a gradual point near the hinge, the section of first growth (technical term, the umbo). In brachiopods, one of their valves will here have an opening in the shell. This hole allows the extrusion of a fleshy stalk-like structure called a pedicle, which would anchor the animal to the sea floor.

The fossils of a soft-bodied worm species have also been found in this location; another group of animals to have ruled these reefs. Some of these were active predators with vicious jaws used to snap up their prey, a feature still seen today in modern bobbit worms. These specially hardened and jagged-edged jaw parts are their most commonly preserved feature (aside from the traces of their burrows in the lime mud), but are typically very small and best seen with a microscope.

Some of these creatures would later evolve to be much larger. Infamously, a Canadian species which lived in the Devonian, *Websteroprion armstrongi*, grew to about one metre in length, one of the biggest worms ever known.

Other top predators were also invertebrates but much stronger built. Large aquatic arthropods called eurypterids (or sea scorpions) patrolled Silurian seas, looking a little like weaponised trilobites. They had segmented bodies with long paddle tails. Their back legs had also evolved into paddles to aid with swimming, whilst their front appendages adapted into ragged claws for catching prey.

These too evolved to be gigantic, with the German *Jaekelopterus* measuring a whopping 2.6 metres in length, making it the largest known arthropod in history (slightly larger than *Arthropleura*). The claws alone would have measured almost half a metre. This group of armoured predators patrolled the shallow seas from the Ordovician (a little over 450 million years ago) until they died out in the Permian mass extinction event (250 million years ago). Eurypterids are rare fossils but are known from UK localities, some of the best discoveries of recent years coming from Portishead.

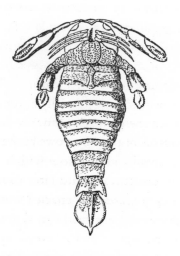

A Eurypterid, commonly known as a sea scorpion

There are some areas of Wenlock Edge that are perceived as being the most productive, such as the old lime-kiln escarpments, but there are actually far more spots out there with fossil-bearing rocks than any brief search will tell you. The group for Regionally Important Geological Sites (RIGS) of Shropshire keeps a database of many such localities, which can be a very useful resource for searching. You can even find loose rocks lying on the floor scattered around parts of the forest around this National Trust park, the bedrock having been partly broken up by tree roots and mixed in with the topsoil.

The Silurian reefs were a distinctly alien marine environment compared to the reefs we know today, just like the Carboniferous forests would later be on the land. Taking something that sounds familiar but flipping it into something truly unique, this is a world that only seems to become stranger the more you examine it.

Cross Hands Quarry

Dipping into the Cotswold hills, the far reaches of Warwickshire are just about as low down the country as you can travel while still being part of the Midlands, though of course, much furious debate often accompanies the classifying of where the Midlands ends and the south begins, so I won't say any more on this before discussing our final site in this region, Cross Hands Quarry.

Cross Hands Quarry is still in use and thus on privately owned land, but you can arrange access by contacting the landowners or by taking part in event visits organised by local geological groups. It can be found along the A44 road, just south of the village of Little Compton.

The rocks of this site yield Jurassic-age limestone (about 167 million years old), making it significantly younger than some of the other Midlands sites we've looked at so far. Seeing as the material is being collected from spoil heaps rather than *in situ* in the ground, much of the material is already broken down into chunks of yellowed stone. Having dealt with Jurassic marine fossils several times before, the regular cast of organisms will be no surprise: the familiar brachiopods, bivalves and crinoids.

Common amongst the shells are more bizarre-looking fossils with a surprising historical connection. The objects in question are shallow-domed circles, reaching almost ten centimetres in diameter, with a light impression on the surface, patterned like a flower. In science we call these fossils *Clypeus plotii*, but a little over two hundred years ago they went by the name 'pound stones'.

This name comes from something we don't often associate with fossils: day-to-day functionality around the house. Long ago, it was noticed that complete *Clypeus* fossils tended to weigh around about one pound (454g) and, seeing as they were so common in the area, they used as a rudimentary standard of measurement. For instance, there are records of pound stones being utilised by dairy farmers as a means of weighing out butter. It raises the interesting thought that the quality of cakes in this part of the world might once have correlated with the baker's skills as a fossil hunter.

After being a curiosity for dairy workers, the pound stones became the focus of scientific revelation in the late eighteenth century. Amongst the keen collectors was an aspiring geologist from Oxfordshire, William Smith, and these fossils were central to his ground-breaking work in map making, which we will revisit at Watchet in the South West (see p.199).

Despite what the patterns on these fossil domes might look like, pound stones are not flowers, but rather, the remains of an ancient species of sea urchins, known to scientists as echinoids, not dissimilar to animals living in the seas today. It is an animal we are familiar with but less immediately apparent out of context and without their bodies being covered in spines, probably the animal's most distinctive feature.

Sea urchins comprise another part of the echinoderms, the major group of animals that includes starfish and crinoids. That flower structure on the top surface is fittingly called the petaloid structures, and they make this urchin odd amongst echinoderms as they give them bilateral symmetry, whereas the majority of echinoderms have radial symmetry. *Clypeus*, and similar species like the living sand dollars, are different from the regular, radial sea urchins and would have spent much of their time burrowing in the substrate, probably for safety from predators.

Beyond echinoids, dinosaur material has also been found at this quarry, though only in small fragmentary finds. The most exciting discovery was made in the 1960s, when fragments of a large theropod dinosaur were unearthed. Very little material was ever collected and therefore this means that any classification is to be taken with a pinch of salt, with the possibility that it may change with new discoveries. For the time being at least, the animal is listed as a unique species amongst the two-legged carnivorous dinosaurs, named *Cruxicheriros*, appropriately meaning 'cross hands'.

No matter where exactly *Cruxicheriros* sits on the dinosaur family tree, it was certainly a large animal, estimated to have been up to nine metres in length. Keep an eye out when looking through the limestone, then, because you may find something which, though perhaps less beautiful, may well have belonged to a rather more spectacular animal.

Not far from the quarry can be found a collection of ancient archaeological monuments: stone circles and standing stones that put into perspective just how far the understanding of the local geology has come. From these mysterious iron-age structures, to using fossils as kitchen accessories, and finally to the industrial applications and scientific discoveries made in the rock today.

East Midlands

Charnwood Forest

Up until now, as we've worked our way down the country, we've seen no fossils older than the Cambrian, about half a billion years ago. In the past, many people took the lack of fossils dating to before this time to mean that life could not have existed before then: that those Cambrian creatures represented some of the very first organisms on earth. It was this confidence that led them to name the Phanerozoic Eon, the eon of life.

If there were places with rocks older than this (grouped under the general term Precambrian), it was common to not bother looking for fossils in them, for none would be found. As such, in 1956, when fifteen-year-old Tina Negus reported to her Geography teacher that she'd spotted fossils in the rocks of Charnwood Forest near Leicester, she was dismissed as having surely seen no more than purely geological features in ancient rocks, not fossils. But Tina would have the last laugh, as we now know that she'd just discovered the oldest evidence of complex life in Europe.

To the south of the forest, the land is dominated by igneous rocks; rugged triangular outcrops of diorite erupt from the ground in clearings, creating an uneven landscape akin to the choppy waters of a rough sea. These rocks will not yield any fossils, however; the famous finds were made deeper into the heart of the forest.

In the centre of the woods, the land rises to form a hill, with larger pinnacles of rock exposed. These are the rocks Tina explored, since assigned to a new geological period called the Ediacaran. Named in 2004 after similar-aged rocks in Australia, this was the first new geological period defined in more than a century. To put an age on the fossils of Charnwood, they're approximately 562 million years old.

Examples of the fossils Tina found can still potentially be found here, though such crucially important discoveries are not to be touched. They're precious to science and should be left in peace; a photographs-only fossil hunt.

It can be very difficult to see the fossils present at Charnwood, which appear as though they're lightly embossed within the rocks. We refer to these fossils as being preserved in low relief, with their structures often only visible under the right lighting and from certain angles. When they do come into focus, what you'll see look rather like fern plants, a repeated patterning of layers in an elongated leaf shape. On first glance, our instinct may be to compare it to a plant, but this is far from the truth of what the organism was. Named *Charnia* for the woods of their discovery, they belong to a group of organisms called rangeomorphs. Though not plants, it is also inaccurate to refer to them as animals, as the truth is that nobody is quite sure how exactly they should be placed on the tree of life as we presently understand it. They are enigmatic fossils but could hold the key to understanding evolution at the very base of the animal family tree, and help to inform us about how complex life first evolved on this planet.

In life, they would have measured around fifteen centimetres and lived in a way akin to modern kelp, anchored to the sea floor by a structure called a holdfast, their frond bodies extending in the water, likely wafting in the current, taking in particulate matter as their food. However, whereas kelp are plants relying on light for their energy, *Charnia* had no such restraints and the dark, fine-grained sediments they are preserved in are typical of a deep marine environment, indicating that they likely grew beyond the range of photosynthesis, with sunlight unable to penetrate to this depth.

Examining them close up, you can observe one of the key features of rangeomorphs; that is, the fact that they have fractal body plans. This basically means that they were composed of repeating structures on smaller scales. As you zoom into the fossil, you'll find that same branching pattern reproduced, increasing their surface area to maximise their ability to collect food.

Similar Ediacaran fossils have been found in other places, most famously at Mistaken Point in Canada. Here, some specimens are thought to have grown up to two metres in length, far dwarfing the fifteen centimetres or so examples of the Charnwood fossils.

One thing separating Charnwood from most other Ediacaran hotspots is the dominance of 'multifoliate' fronds here; that is to say, species with multiple fronds emanating from a single holdfast. It seems that in this area in particular there was a large diversity of different body plans. We are learning more and more about the intriguing secrets of these

Ediacarans, thanks to the work of brilliant scientists like Dr Frankie Dunn, whose enthusiasm for these bizarre fronds is enough to make you question why dinosaurs hog so much of the palaeontological spotlight.

Many of the key specimens of *Charnia* have since been removed from Charnwood for study, but some remain, and there is always the possibility of new discoveries being made. To guarantee spotting some, though, it may be best to go to a museum. The original specimen can be seen on display in the New Walk Museum in Leicester.

Tilton-on-the-Hill

England is not known for mountains in the same way as Scotland or Wales. Aside from a few spots in the north, it is a generally flatter country. A map showing the height of ground above sea level will reveal that the East Midlands and Anglia are just about the flattest regions of the UK, a fact those of us from hillier parts might sometimes find ourselves envious of. That isn't to say it's a vast expanse of level ground akin to the outback of Australia, as there are still places where the ground rises, with one of the highest points south-east of the Peak District, a few miles outside Leicester. The actual highest location is a relic of sorts, the former village of Whatborough, which was cleared away in 1495. Between this medieval settlement and modern-day Tilton-on-the-Hill lies our next fossil-hunting location.

The reason for focusing on these hills is due to the fact that their very existence is responsible for the creation of the site in the first place. Extending perpendicular to Oakham Road is a designated nature reserve for birds and an array of ferns running through the uniform agricultural land; a shallow valley with walls of exposed rock slowly being overrun by plants. This is not a natural exposure, but an area created to facilitate the construction of a railway line in the 1870s.

This is the Tilton Railway Cutting, one of a great number of sites around the UK that owe their origin to such industrial expansion. Train tracks, roads and general constructions work best along smooth, level surfaces (something rarely found in nature). When building, if there is a hill that is too steep to be traversed, then a flatter pathway is gouged out of the rock, creating a cutting. We pass these all the time and don't often pay them attention, though they loom, like miniature cliffs along roadways.

Creating these requires excavations that often involve digging straight through beds of rock potentially rich in fossils, exposing layers of strata that the average palaeontologist would not otherwise have the ability (and certainly not the permission) to access.

The reason for the focus on this particular cutting is two-fold. The first is the obvious: unsurprisingly, rock valleys excavated for train tracks usually have trains running through them, making access impossible and stupidly dangerous. Here at Tilton, however, the line has been out of use since 1965, a victim of the infamous Beeching cuts (the plan to increase the efficiency of the UK's nationalised rail system that resulted in mass closures across the country), resulting in far greater accessibility.

The second reason is that not many cuttings can boast having a genus of fossil named after them. The rock on show is predominantly ironstone, dating to the early Jurassic, around 190 million years old, and preserves a diverse group of shelled marine invertebrates, including the eponymous ammonite, *Tiltoniceras*.

This ammonite was once common in these cuttings but is now a rarer find. It can be identified by looking at the inner spiral, which should be smooth, without strong growth lines, ribs or tubercles.

Brachiopods are the most common fossils here now, such as *Tetrarhynchia*, which has a classic brachiopod shape. The shell is curved and heavily ribbed, the smooth edge of the shell where the valves meet jutting out to form a notch in the centre. Such invertebrate finds commonly erode out of the strata.

Not being a natural cliff, without anything as efficient as the coastal winds and tide to keep the rock surfaces fresh, they are slowly being reclaimed by the wild plants. One of the predominant forms of weathering here is biological, with plant roots forcing their way into the fissures of the rock. Never underestimate the power of plants, as their growth fractures the rock, causing them to split along pre-existing lines of weakness. Fortunately for us, these lines are often caused by the presence of fossils, and this is one of the reasons that shells can be found so intact here, having literally popped out the rock.

Getting to this cutting can be tricky, as it isn't broadly signposted and there aren't public transport options, making driving the only choice. Travelling from Tilton, the cutting is found shortly before the turning for Hyde Lodge Road, with limited parking available. A small sign displaying the history of the site is found before a pathway to the valley beneath.

Waiting until they've been retired from use is one way to gain access to the fossils of these cuttings. The other is to be part of them being made. Cuttings like this are still created in construction today, and the companies will sometimes bring on board palaeontological consultants to advise on whether the rocks they're moving through contain anything of scientific value. During this process, there can be occasions where access to the spoil heaps is open for amateur fossil hunters to aid in the search, though this is very rare.

Joining such events can only ever be done through local scientific groups or industry contacts and is not something that can be signed up for on a whim.

It should also be stated that such important finds on expeditions like this are, by default, the property of the organisation behind the search, not your own, thus ensuring they rightfully end up in museums. But the opportunity of adventure and the chance to find unique discoveries makes them more than worthwhile.

Irchester

In the woods above Northampton, there are huge dinosaur skeletons amongst the trees. But before you get your hopes up, it's worth mentioning that these are not fossils, but in fact wooden climbing frames for children in Irchester Country Park. Their placement isn't entirely random, however. Though now an activity centre, it was built on the site of a formerly fossil-bearing quarry, and there are still some exposures you can collect from today.

Like with many other quarries, it was the rich ironstone deposits that drove the mining activity. A museum of steam locomotives on the site provides more information on the human history of the area, as well as some of the original engines and mining equipment.

Of all the area's exposures where the scree can still yield fossils, the most popular of these is Wembley Pit, within the grounds of the park. Here, the strata is predominantly a yellowed limestone from the Jurassic period, around 175 million years old. As is always the case with such material, what you will find preserved are organisms of a marine ecosystem, relics of the ancient shallow sea that covered the UK during this period. Shelly fossils are the most common find, along with more echinoids, like those seen at Cross Hands Quarry (see p.148).

Trace fossils of worm burrows are particularly common here too; those wriggling lines clearly contrasting with the base colour of the rock. Much of the rock itself is interesting, made of a 'bubbly' texture you regularly see in limestones. The scientific term ascribed to this is oolitic, with each of those tiny spheres of limestone known as an ooid. Each ooid forms like a snowball, with individual grains rolled around on the sea floor, building up layers of lime mud. Countless numbers of these spheres gathered together come to form this type of limestone.

Some of the common body fossils here are a group that does often appear in the rocks of other localities, but one we haven't had an opportunity to explore in detail until now:

the gastropods. This is the group commonly referred to as the slugs and snails. Though they have come in many diverse forms over time, their basic body plan has stayed much the same for millions of years (with features like their shells easily recognisable in their dinosaur-age contemporaries).

Like their fellow spiral-shelled molluscs, the ammonites, a snail's hardened shell gives it a natural advantage when it comes to fossilisation, being composed of calcium carbonate (chemically similar in composition to the limestone they're found in).

Gastropods are regularly classified by the shape of their shells, based on the structure of coils (whorls) in the shell. Due to the sheer number of specialist terms that exist for describing snail structure, we will cover only a few of the more basic ones here.

A gastropod with a cone-turret whorled shell

Typically, gastropod shells are regular spirals, like those of the garden snails we know today, but some are narrow and coil sharply to form long, tightly wound shells like turrets (turbinate or turriform shells). If the opposite is true, and all the coiling is flatter to the surface, on a plane, it is known as planispiral. There are also unique shapes like the obconic shells (seen in cone snails) and the flatter, whorless patellate shape of limpets.

One of the more distinct turret-shelled genera you can find in Irchester is the *Aphanoptyxis*, usually around four centimetres in length and with very clear ridges along the shell. The prevalence of this specific gastropod was part of the reasoning behind the Old Lodge Pit being listed as a SSSI. This nearby site yields similar finds to Wembley Pit but is harder to access, and flooding here can be more of an issue.

There are other sites near Irchester to have produced similar finds, though these aren't as accessible. Best known of these is probably Finedon Top Lodge Quarry, which has produced a large abundance of the ridged brachiopod, *Sharpirhynchia*. Like the graptolites that we discussed previously, this brachiopod of the Middle Jurassic has been used as an important index fossil to define sections of geological time, and is named after the Victorian scientist who first proposed this stratigraphic method, Samuel Sharp.

Wembley Pit is by far the easiest fossil location to explore in Irchester, located as it is in an area well stocked with amenities and parking, designed specifically for day-trip visitors. In order to ensure the safe usage and sustainability of the site, any visitors are required to inform the park rangers of their intent to collect at this location, with contact details found easily on the website. You don't need any special permissions to discover the massive wooden dinosaurs, however.

East Anglia

Hunstanton

Defining precise layers in cliff strata can sometimes be a tricky job, picking out the slight variations in colour and texture in mostly grey rock that all too often blend together once you are more than a few metres away. But that is certainly not a problem you will encounter at Hunstanton Beach, our first fossil site of East Anglia. There is no other site mentioned in this book where the boundary between the major rock units is more pronounced than here.

For one and a half kilometres, the shore is marked by sheer cliffs of red sandstone, the high iron-oxide content of the rock giving it a particularly vivid red colouration. But that only accounts for the lower two-thirds of the cliffs, and nearer to the top, the rock suddenly and dramatically shifts to white chalk. Though this chalk is somewhat iron-stained, the difference is still striking. It looks to all the world as though someone were tasked with painting the cliffs but ran out of paint after a few hours. The area owes most of its popularity to these beautiful cliffs, but there is more to them than just aesthetics, they're also full of fossils.

Fossils can be found here from both colour bands, with both also dated to the same time period, the Cretaceous. The lower rocks are about 100 million years old, whilst the chalk above is approximately 9 million years younger. As we move down the country, we still largely see the general trend of moving forward in time. It is far from perfect, with those older patches still cropping up, but overall, the exposures here are younger than what we've seen before.

These rocks produce plentiful brachiopods, sponges, bivalves and belemnites, representing a diverse marine community. Ammonites are also a regular find from the red beds, with most of the fossils coming from one layer of limestone (giving it a red colouration that may blend in with the surrounding sandstone).

Another find you might come across here are echinoids (sea urchins), though here you'll find that not all echinoids have the same general look of the Midlands' pound stones. In fact, that particular body plan is known as being an irregular echinoid. What we call regular echinoids are still sea urchins, but their fossil remains are very different. These echinoids are known as 'regular' because of their symmetry, like so many things in biology. Being part of the echinoderm phylum, it is the usual condition for them to have radial symmetry in their bodies; regular echinoids have this, irregular do not. Instead of a domed, slightly heart-shaped body, a regular echinoid is closer to being spherical. Rather than the 'flower' pattern on the top side, these regular species have vertical banding, split up like an uneven beach ball, alternating narrow and wide bands. The sphere may well be ornamented with protruding hemispheres, giving it a knobbly appearance. Those bumpy circles are actually where the spines of the sea urchin attached themselves; after all, today's urchins have bodies that look just like these fossils, only they're hidden under hundreds of sharp spines for deterring predators.

The reason spines aren't often found with the bodies is not because the spines themselves don't fossilise but because it's rare for them to stay attached post-mortem. Spines are actually extremely common in the fossil record, and you may well come across countless examples of them as you hunt. They can be recognised by their perfectly cylindrical shape, looking exactly as they do in life (just fragmented and very small, so either easily missed or not worth collecting).

In the rare event that they're found intact, they're usually flattened, preserved closer to being a disc of spines shining out of the central body like a halo. Not all spines follow these rules, though. Some species have evolved exceptionally odd spines, such as the truly bizarre *Tylocidaris* echinoids, which have spines that look more like baseball bats.

The narrow bands of the echinoids show us where the animal had rows of soft tube-like feet, which helped them to move (being able to use suction to grip a surface in a way the spines cannot) and have uses in respiration. They also can be used to transport food to their mouths, which is usually seen in the fossil as a hole at the convergence point of all the bands, though in rare cases the mouth parts can also preserve.

A popular tourist attraction and immediately next to the town itself, Hunstanton is very easy to access and fossils can be found from the loose rocks up and down the beach right up to where the cliffs suddenly give way to open sands. There's plenty to see here even on a day of few fossils, with the beach being home to the decaying wreck of a steam trawler, an almost two-hundred-year-old picturesque lighthouse (on a site used since the seventeenth century), and of course the cliffs themselves.

Deep History Coast

Beyond Hunstanton, the coastline of Norfolk is dubbed as an Area of Outstanding Natural Beauty with massive level sands and dune systems; a haven for wading seabirds that rely on sifting out their invertebrate prey from the mudflats. Several reserves around here are top picks for birdwatchers, but to a palaeontologist it may seem a little empty. Flat, sandy beaches aren't ideal for fossil opportunities. As you move east, you'll eventually find the area known as the Deep History Coast, and that's a name with palaeontological promise.

On this 22-mile stretch, the oldest fossils you're likely to find are a mere two million years old, hardly true deep time compared to those fossils to be found elsewhere in the country. But actually, the most interesting stuff of all comes from only a few hundred thousand years ago (which by this point should sound very recent indeed) and is centred around the coast of West Runton.

The strata you find here are predominantly sands and mudstones, with a few deposits of glacial boulder clay. This is an indication of the kind of environment the UK was experiencing less than a million years ago. It was the Ice Age, and West Runton has revealed specimens of some truly iconic species from this time.

Being so close to the modern day, many of the animal remains that can be found may be familiar, including some deer species. Others have since disappeared from Britain but are attempting a comeback through re-introduction schemes, such as the wild boar. The real stars, though, are those animals that may well be the most famous extinct creatures from outside the Mesozoic: the Ice Age megafauna.

Megafauna is a word used by palaeontologists to describe very large animals, and in Ice Age Britain it's mostly used in reference to two groups of animals: prehistoric rhinoceros and mammoths. The remains of both have been discovered at West Runton.

Most famous of all was a discovery made here in 1990, when a nearly complete skeleton of an enormous elephant was extracted, carefully and slowly, from the Pleistocene strata. The species was identified as *Mammuthus trogontherii*, better known as the steppe mammoth.

The word mammoth is usually associated specifically with the thick-haired woolly mammoths, but the diversity of these ancient elephants extended far beyond just them (though they too can be found in Pleistocene deposits in Britain). In fact, a steppe mammoth was far bigger, and would have towered over a typical member of its furry relatives. They would also have had substantially less hair. The mammoth of West Runton would have measured four metres in height (a full metre taller than most woollies) and weighed about as much as two African elephants.

They're named for the habitat they ruled, a 'steppe' being a large area of open grassland. But the British Isles themselves would have been more wooded than a typical steppe, so how would these animals have had enough room to live and feed? There's also the question of how such large animals came to be here in the first place.

The answers to both of these questions are found by reconstructing the past geography of the area. Although the positions of the world's countries were the same in the Ice Age as they are now, the available landmass was very different. With so much water locked away in ice, and with the effects of glacier weight, the sea levels of the Pleistocene were far lower, and what today is the south-east coast of the UK was then connected to what is now northern France, Belgium and the Netherlands by a vast expanse of low-lying grasslands called 'Doggerland'. This was the land that supported these massive herds of megafauna and allowed them to move freely between continental Europe and the British Isles.

It's estimated that the last remnants of this landmass survived until less than ten thousand years ago, when the final few islands of greenery were submerged under the North Sea. But the remains of many animals still lie buried under the surface and can wash up on our shores.

Mammoth remains are the most sought after by palaeontologists, with their teeth being particularly identifiable. These teeth are light in colour, up to fifteen centimetres long and notable for their distinct grooves. They will be smooth on the sides, though the top will appear as rows of slightly wobbly (but overall parallel) lines. This was the chewing surface used to grind up plant food. Large bone material and tusks are prized finds, but often highly fragile. These ancient tusks are usually especially unstable and likely to literally explode, cracking and shedding layers if not looked after correctly.

Though the remains of this megafauna can be found here, the truly impressive finds are rare, and you're more likely to come across unidentifiable bone fragments if you're lucky enough to see mammal remains. Ice Age megafauna is largely known around the UK from cave deposits, which are inaccessible to all but the most experienced cavers. The finds of cave deposits can be incredible, showing a world simultaneously close to our own and unimaginably different; a Britain filled with cave bears, big cats and giant deer (the biggest being *Megaloceros*, whose antlers were as wide as an African elephant is tall).

The Deep History Coast is expansive, with plenty of information to be found here telling you the stories behind the beaches. Best accessed via West Runton and the on-site car park there, further along the beaches you can find archaeological heritage, including some of the UK's most ancient stone tools and human footprints. After all, it wasn't only mammoths that made the walk across Doggerland to first reach these lands.

Beyond the beaches, just off the coast, is also a natural wonder that has been lovingly referred to as 'Norfolk's Great Barrier Reef', the Cromer Shoal Chalk Beds. This marine conservation zone is the largest chalk reef in Europe and home to hundreds of species, some unique to this particular system. It's an ecosystem built upon Cretaceous rocks carved by Ice Age glacial activity; a community of fossils now supporting life. The name of the Deep History Coast seems highly apt.

The Amber Coast

Ammonites, trilobites and dinosaur bones are all fossil icons, but there is another member of this group quite unlike the rest. Capable of preserving the finest details of animals, amber adds a splash of brilliant golden colour to the palaeontological world so often dominated by the rather uninspiring palate of blacks, greys and whites.

Historically valued for its beauty as a jewellery component, the alternative view of amber exploded into prominence thanks to a certain popular science-fiction franchise – Jurassic Park. It's fair to say that that story might have exaggerated many aspects of what can be achieved with amber, but there is some truth behind the fantasy.

Unlike other precious gemstones like diamonds, amber is not forged in the depths of the earth, but created organically by living things. This is the part of the science that Jurassic Park does get correct: amber is the fossilised remnants of tree sap. Travelling through specialised channels within the trunks, sap is like the 'blood' of trees, transporting sugars and minerals from the roots to the farthest branches.

If sap breaks to the surface, its sweet scent is irresistible to insects, hopeful for a quick meal. Unfortunately for them, the liquid is viscous and sticky, meaning that many who set foot in it are unable to ever escape. Some are completely enveloped by the sap and are frozen in time; cut off and protected from the world, they're preserved in extraordinary detail. Those mosquitoes seen in the films with even their delicate wing membranes visible are something not only possible, but observable in the fossil record.

This is where the accuracy of Jurassic Park ends, however. There are countless problems with the idea of DNA extraction from these specimens, not least because DNA only survives in any 'readable' form for a matter of thousands of years, far too short a span to reach the dinosaurs.

Even without DNA, though, amber is incredible, giving an unprecedented window into life far more detailed than regular fossils provide. Even more amazingly, insects aren't the only creatures preserved, as the sap can also ensnare vertebrates. Frogs and lizards have been discovered within the golden capsules, and one of the most unbelievable finds of recent years was a section of a (notably tiny) dinosaur tail.

Amber is often thought of as originating in tropical mines, and indeed some of the discoveries mentioned above have heralded from the amber mines of Myanmar, all of which are highly controversial due to the human-rights violations associated with them. But in fact, a large percentage of amber comes from Lithuania. The Baltic is an incredibly rich source of fossil sap, with what is now a sea having previously been a forest, home to a myriad of life in the Eocene epoch, 40 million years ago.

Denmark and Sweden are just two of the barriers between us and the Baltic, but the seaway route is not completely closed off, and amber from this ancient woodland can still gather in substantial quantities in the North Sea before washing up on our shores. Nowhere is that amber more commonly found than the stretch of coast between Felixstowe and Southwold, earning it the nickname 'The Amber Coast'.

When cleaned up and prepared for display, the amber found here is the rich colour we are used to, bright and translucent. However, don't expect to find it looking so pristine on the beach. In its 'wild' form, amber is a rougher, darker brown hue, the outer layer obscured by the weathering and imperfections from its time in the sea. In some cases, a slight windowing can still be seen, and you can identify the subject by holding it up to the light and looking for the amber shine. In other cases, it really can be almost indistinguishable from the surrounding pebbles. As with any kind of fossil hunting, identifying it takes practice.

One difference you might note is that amber has a very different feel to it than a regular rock. Amber is lighter and, on fresh surfaces, can almost feel like man-made plastic, though admittedly these traits are hard to detect in smaller samples, which is what you are most likely to discover.

Even though this is the best place to find amber in Britain, it still doesn't make it common. Discovering any size trace of the fossil resin amongst the shingle is cause for celebration.

The Naze

As we continue that general de-ageing trend of the rocks as we move south-east, in Anglia there are plentiful exposures of rock from the Cenozoic. This is the era of time after the extinction of the dinosaurs (66 million years ago), and stretches all the way to the modern day (the Cenozoic is the era which we ourselves are currently in). Gone are the giant reptiles that once ruled the lands; this is the time of mammals, and a far more familiar landscape, all of which is preserved in the crag.

In most parts of the UK, the word 'crag' doesn't refer to any one type of stone in particular, instead being a general term for a rough outcrop of rock. As such, it is a word often linked with climbing. In the south-east, however, the word has a more specific definition. Here, a crag is a particular formation of rock packed with fossilised seashells. The most fossiliferous of these is the fittingly named Red Crag, easy to identify from its vibrant colour, also to be seen staining those shells preserved within it.

This colour makes identifying layers fairly easy in strata along the coast such as at the Naze; the grey rocks there belonging to the London Clay of the Eocene (54 million years ago), whereas the Red Crag is far more recent, dated to the Pliocene, only 3.3 million years ago. When those Pliocene fossils were alive, early humans were rising in the African Rift Valley, the birthplace of our species. It may be closer to the modern day, but the fact that we still find seashells in a place that is now dry land makes clear the fact that we remain a fair way from the world we know now.

Across the recent Cenozoic epochs, the climate was changing rapidly. The poles were freezing, locking up fresh water and reducing global sea levels. Long ago was the period when the UK was made up of tropical islands; the country is now a larger land mass located roughly in our current position to the north. This retreating sea can be evidenced in locations like the Buckanay Farm Pit near Alderton, where it is recorded in ripple sequences in the strata, alongside classic Red Crag fossils.

Of all those usual shells found in the Red Crag of Anglia, there is one find in particular which the Naze alone can claim. Every year, enthusiasts come here in the hope that they might find one of the holy grails for fossil hunters. An instantly recognisable shape, these triangles of rock can be the size of your hand. They have a smooth texture on the surface up to the apex, with a thicker and rounded mass at the base. You don't need training in anatomy to see that it's a shark tooth, though this is one unlike any you'll find in living creatures. This fossil originated in one of the most infamous fish ever to swim the seas, *megalodon*, and the Naze is the one of the only places in the UK these teeth have ever been discovered.

Picture a large predatory shark today and you'll imagine a Great White, a beautiful fish stuck with a nasty reputation. The largest great white shark ever confirmed is the 6-metre individual nicknamed 'Deep Blue'; in contrast, it's thought *megalodon* could grow more than fifty feet in length, over twice the size.

The exact body plan of a living *megalodon* is largely theoretical, but recent research led by Dr Catalina Pimiento and Jack Cooper of the University of Swansea has suggested that *megalodon* had at least the same basic tail structure of a great white, with a dorsal fin the size of a full-grown human. This giant size may well have been its undoing, as competition from smaller species, toothed whales, and the loss of many of its preferred prey species are thought to have contributed to *megalodon*'s extinction about three million years ago.

Although it did live in the seas until fairly recently in palaeontological terms, the *megalodon* is most assuredly extinct, despite what certain corners of pop-culture might like to imply. You are perfectly safe to venture into the waters without fear of attack from a 15-metre-long shark. Even if it were to co-exist with us, it would be far more interested in hunting larger seagoing mammals such as whales and dolphins, and would likely ignore us completely.

Be careful not to get too swept up in the mythical status that *megalodon* holds, and remember that, just because their teeth can be found, they are by no means common. Finds of these teeth are rare enough that, on a slow news day, they've been deemed worthy of reporting on local news. Visiting the Naze won't guarantee you a giant shark tooth, but the abundance and preservation of fossils in this classic UK location will certainly keep you satisfied. There are plenty of interesting invertebrates here too, such as the unusual gastropod *Neptunea angulata*.

Thanks to the Red Crag being such a soft-rock formation, it is rapidly eroding, meaning plenty of fossils are regularly washed out onto the shore, commonly freed from surrounding sediment. Often you can crumble the matrix away with your hands when discovering the seashells of the Naze, without any real need for hammering.

The best site is near the town of Walton-on-the-Naze, beginning from around the 26-metre Naze Tower (also a good place to park up), and walking beyond the sea wall to the coast opening up in front of you, a sandy shore scattered with boulders fallen from the low slumping cliffs.

South-East England

Stonesfield

Stonesfield is a small, unassuming village in the county of Oxfordshire and, to look at it today, few would guess the enormous contribution this area paid not only to science, but to human culture in general.

The outskirts of this settlement formerly hosted the Stonesfield Slate Mine, a common resource for building materials in the Midlands during the early nineteenth century. Primarily used for roofing, the site produced great quantities of Jurassic limestone, dating to about 167 million years ago.

At the time the quarry was active, the science of palaeontology was only just finding its feet, and places like Stonesfield were prime spots for pioneer fossil hunters. One of the most common visitors to this particular site was William Buckland. Having already made a name for himself by collecting ancient wolf and bear remains in cave deposits, in 1822 it was here that he made the biggest discovery of his life.

From the limestone, he uncovered a single lower jawbone (dentary) belonging to a reptile, only this bone was almost 30 cm in length, and showed several huge teeth mounted within it. Along with the jaw came parts of a shoulder blade, and large sections of a back leg, including partial hip. They could only have belonged to a predator of enormous size. The creature was dubbed *Megalosaurus*; Buckland had just discovered and formally identified a dinosaur for the very first time in history.

By no means was Buckland the first to stumble on a dinosaur bone, however; cultures the world over have been finding and interpreting them since humans came to be. It's thought that dinosaurs could well have been the inspiration behind certain myths in Ancient Greece, and some Native American cultures even recognised that these bones were the remains of beasts that roamed the earth long in the past. What *Megalosaurus* represents is the beginning of the classification of dinosaurs as we understand them today.

That said, imaginations ran wild at first, and it would be a long time before reconstructions caught up with what we would now recognise as a dinosaur. Initial attempts at piecing together these creatures looked more like crosses between crocodiles and elephants, huge models of which can still be seen in all their glory at Crystal Palace Park in London.

This enduring image of dinosaurs as sluggish reptilian giants was challenged majorly in the late 1960s, in a time dubbed the 'dinosaur renaissance'. This was the time when the link between dinosaurs and birds became more evident, and science realised how active and agile they could have been. The famous pictures of lumbering giants would be replaced with images of dinosaurs with fast-paced lives. *Megalosaurus* was going through an image change.

We now know *Megalosaurus* to be a theropod, the group of two-legged carnivorous dinosaurs like *Dracoraptor* (see p.119). It possessed long and powerful hind legs, and shorter forearms, each hand with three sharply clawed fingers. Standing two and a half metres tall and nine metres from snout to tail, *Megalosaurus* was a top predator of Jurassic dinosaurs in Britain.

Megalosaurus may have been the first named, but an avalanche of discoveries was not far behind. At first, nobody had any idea just how diverse and species-rich dinosaurs were, so it was often the case that, whenever a new large fossil was found, it had a good chance of being immediately assigned to *Megalosaurus*. After all, what other animal could possibly have bones so enormous? This inevitably led to many animals being mistakenly labelled, making early collections a bit of a mess, with experts unsure as to what is and isn't correctly labelled. This is especially problematic when information giving context of the discovery is lost (a reminder of how important it is to keep this for your own collections).

The Stonesfield Slate Mine, birthplace of our modern dinosaur fanaticism, was long-hailed as one of the best fossil locations in the country. However, to visit it now, instead of open rock, you will find farmhouses and fields. The mines closed long ago, and there is little indication of the enormous significance of the site, though the original *Megalosaurus* fossils can be viewed in the Oxford University Museum of Natural History. Collecting opportunities may be lacking here now, but in this journey of UK palaeontology, this former Oxfordshire mine played one of the biggest roles of all, and thus demands a mention.

Tilgate Forest

The story of palaeontology and Tilgate Forest is one frequently retold in the history of science. This begins with Mary Ann Mantell and her husband Gideon going for a walk in 1822. The story goes that, whilst her surgeon husband was visiting a patient, a small rock by the pathside caught Mary's eye. In it, she found a smooth brown fossil with a curved and ridged shape. Immediately the pair embarked on a quest to identify it, going as far as to send it to famed French naturalist Georges Cuvier. But even that palaeontological pioneer failed to get it right, assuming it came from a rhinoceros.

In 1825, at last, a paper was released with a fantastically long title that probably could have stopped after the first four words: 'Notice on the *Iguanodon*'. In this paper, the fossil was identified as coming from a large herbivorous reptile, the name based on the tooth's shape, similar to that of a modern iguana. This comparison is shown in the very first attempt to reconstruct the animal, which had it positioned much like a lizard clinging onto a (presumably enormous) tree branch. We now recognise *Iguanodon* as being the second formal identification of a dinosaur.

Those initial recreations happened to feature one of the most famous mistakes in palaeontology. Of course, there are plenty to choose from in early efforts, but people regularly point to the top of the *Iguanodon* snout, on which has been drawn a small horn, akin to a newborn crocodile's egg tooth. It would later be revealed this wasn't a horn at all, but a thumb spike on the animal's forelimb.

There are a few theories on the purpose of this conical spike, with the most commonly depicted being usage in defence, attempting to injure a large attacker. A less exciting but probably more common use was that it could be used for digging up plant matter on which the animal could feed. But if you have a soft spot for the bulky and monstrously horned reconstruction, it too is represented by huge sculptures in Crystal Palace Park, along with *Megalosaurus* and a multitude of marine reptiles.

At the time of the discovery, *Iguanodon* was unlike almost anything known to science, with it and *Megalosaurus* existing in a league of their own. Then, just a few years later at another quarry around Tilgate Forest, a new mystery emerged. These bones were from a clearly different species (named *Hylaeosaurus*) and provided a greater insight into the skeletal structure of the animals. These spectacular finds demanded the establishment of a new group terminology, and so, in 1842, the word 'dinosaur' was coined to describe them by Sir Richard Owen, the first director of the Natural History Museum.

Iguanodon was a large herbivore of the Cretaceous (around 130 million years ago) and it is one of the most commonly found dinosaurs in Britain (or at least the most commonly reported of the large remains). In life, it was probably predominantly bipedal, though the forelimb structure suggests it could have moved on four legs to help feed low to the ground.

The skull featured bountiful tooth rows at the back of the jaw, but a completely toothless front, where it would have had a beak structure for nipping at plants. This unique arrangement allowed *Iguanodon* to chew food, a simple skill few dinosaurs possessed. Most dinosaurs would simply swallow food chunks whole, like birds, with large herbivores swallowing stones to grind up the food in their stomachs. These stones can still be found today and are known as gastroliths (but they are very rare and unlikely to be found and positively identified in the UK).

Multiple lineages are seen innovating eating styles in the Cretaceous, largely due to the evolution of a remarkable new group of organisms. The later Mesozoic saw the explosive arrival of a major group of plants we can't imagine the world without: flowers and grasses. It is only in the Cretaceous that we start to see the foliage of the planet starting to become more recognisable to us, and animals were evolving to take advantage, a time known as the Cretaceous Terrestrial Revolution.

Herbivorous dinosaurs took advantage of this, but none adapted as significantly as certain insect groups. With no flowers until now, there had been no pollinating insects. Insect fossils are rare anyway, but before this time there were no traces of bees or butterflies, both of which could only now evolve and diversify. Though grasses had now evolved, they wouldn't truly dominate the globe until after the Cretaceous extinction event.

The quarries surrounding Tilgate Forest where these dinosaur rocks originated (such as Whiteman's Green) are long since overgrown or built over. Though a few outcrops remain, you are very unlikely to find anything in them. Much like Stonesfield, the story of Tilgate Forest is mentioned for its importance in the story of UK palaeontology, and you couldn't write a book on the fossils of Britain without mentioning it.

Smokejack Clay Pit

Smokejack Clay Pit is on private land, but still sometimes accessible to the public for fossil hunting. This is commonly done through groups granted special permission, such as the UK Association of Fossil Hunters, who have in the past run guided hunts with their members. The site itself is located next to Somersbury Wood, though any visit here must first be cleared with the landowners.

The pit is large, taking up fifty-six hectares, and looks exactly as one might imagine a former open-pit quarry to look: a basin of steeply sloping rock walls. The most interesting layers for fossils are fairly near the top, where the predominantly grey strata give way to more yellows and browns. Here the rock is dated to around 128 million years ago, still in the Cretaceous. This is part of the Wealden Clay, and is prime territory for discovering dinosaurs.

The findings here suggest that it was once a kind of wetlands environment, as indicated by the fish and crocodile remains that can be found here. Crocodile teeth are probably the most common reptile find at Smokejack, but dinosaurs do appear as well. That most common of British Cretaceous dinosaurs, *Iguanodon* (see p.178), has been discovered here, along with several other species.

The stories of the most amazing discoveries often begin humbly, with a few fragments of discoloured bone protruding from a slightly suspicious lump of rock. Occasionally, though, these first finds are breathtakingly impressive, as was the case for amateur fossil hunter William J. Walker when exploring the Smokejack Clay Pit in 1983.

Even with all of the incredible other remains coming out of the quarry, there is one animal in particular all visitors want to find, inspired by that 1983 discovery. What Walker picked up here was a vicious-looking 28-centimetre curved claw, a serious piece of weaponry from a presumably formidable dinosaur. Calling on experts from the Natural History Museum to help, what was eventually excavated was a giant predator, dubbed *Baryonyx walkeri*.

Baryonyx was part of a popular group of dinosaurs called the spinosaurs, recognisable from their elongated, crocodilian skulls. *Baryonyx* was no exception to this, measuring nearly a metre from the tip of the snout to the start of the neck. Large arms framed that impressive hooked weapon, one monster claw on the first finger of each hand. These terrifying features gave it its name, meaning 'heavy claw' (with *walkeri* added in homage to the discoverer).

At first, you could think that these vicious talons might suggest the *Baryonyx* being an apex predator, hunting other dinosaurs, but in truth, they point to a more specialist lifestyle. The claws, teeth and snout are all perfect adaptations for catching fish, though the discovery of other *Baryonyx* teeth with herbivorous dinosaur remains at this very site mean the idea of these large predators feasting on larger prey can't be ruled out.

The most infamous member of the spinosaur group was the eponymous *Spinosaurus*, which is to date the largest theropod dinosaur ever discovered – the idea of *T. rex* being the largest is a common misconception. *Spinosaurus* is well known for the two-metre-tall sail on its back, a feature not present in *Baryonyx*. Fully adapting to the life of a fisher, research led by Dr Nizar Ibrahim in 2020 suggested that *Spinosaurus* was more aquatic than many of its relatives, even possessing a large paddle-like tail that some have likened to a newt.

If dinosaurs aren't your thing, then this site can provide more of the smaller scale of life, as the clay pit has churned up some of the best-preserved fossil insects in the country. Seven orders of insect have been described from this single location, found most often near the base of the quarry exposure. Plant remains of ferns and conifers which grew in these marshy conditions can also be discovered here.

Cretaceous crustaceans can also be found at Smokejack. Though the crustaceans are an ancient group of organisms, the true crabs as we know them today didn't appear until the mid- to late-Mesozoic era, following a 'revolution' in the marine ecosystem, which saw a great deal of diversification in water-dwelling invertebrates.

Isle of Sheppey

The fossil-hunting world is associated most with the Mesozoic: dinosaurs, marine reptiles and ammonites, or else the Palaeozoic trilobites or recent Ice Age megafauna. Those millions of years between the end of the Cretaceous and the Ice Age are amongst the most overlooked in the fossil world. One area where this substantial block of time hasn't been forgotten, though, is on the Isle of Sheppey. This is possibly the best place in the country to find fossils from the Eocene epoch (56 to 34 million years ago).

There are a handful of sites dotted around this 36-square-mile island near the Thames Estuary, but one of the most celebrated sites for fossil hunting is on the coast to the north, from Minster-on-Sea to Warden Point.

The largest things you're likely to discover here are huge slabs of concrete and ruined structures. Certainly not pre-historic, remains of an artillery battery and massive sound reflector from World War Two litter the shoreline at Warden Point. Beyond them, from the brown cliffs of Sheppey, can be found fossils of animals that lived in the seas, only recently recovered from the asteroid impact, in a geological formation called the London Clay.

Though some bone fragments and teeth can be found loose and free from the rock, the best fossils are in the hardened nodules, which can contain fossils with extraordinary three-dimensional preservation. Some of these can be completely hidden away inside, but often you can catch a glimpse of what might be within them from the dark black colouration of the fossils contrasting with the lighter matrix.

Amongst the finest fossils of this ecosystem is a major group of animals we have so far only encountered in passing, despite their enormous global significance, as the beaches of Sheppey are an amazing place to find the remains of crustaceans.

Crustaceans are a hugely diverse group and always have been, with fossils dating back to the Cambrian, placing them amongst the first arthropod groups to diversify. Many ancient forms looked much like the shrimp and lobsters of today, with crabs evolving in the Mesozoic from their lobster-like ancestors through a process dubbed carcinisation, an evolutionary model in which an organism evolves to become more crab-like in shape. In the case of crustaceans, this hiding of the tail under the body gives added protection and removes a potential target spot that predators might otherwise take advantage of.

Crabs of the London Clay at Sheppey are recognisable thanks to their resemblance to the modern crabs we are familiar with and are easy to distinguish if you have enough of them preserved. The most common genus here is probably *Zanthopsis*, the body of which looks much the same as a small edible crab from today.

Even if you aren't lucky enough to find complete specimens, fragmentary crustacean remains are recognisable. The claws and jointed legs are usually clear enough. The main shell body of a crustacean is the carapace, often showing a distinct bumpy texture, as you see in living examples. Even with only these fragments, identification can be possible, as many crustaceans can be recognised from the various distinctive grooves in their carapace.

Lobsters are also present here, featuring many of the same features of the crabs but usually with narrower carapaces and a segmented tail behind them. This tail is often preserved curled beneath their bodies, the same being true for shrimp.

Crustaceans belong to the arthropods, the single most diverse group of animals on the planet, with a rich and extensive fossil history, though they can at times be exceptionally hard to spot in the field. Some, like beetles, have evolved into a mind-blowing variety of forms of different shapes, sizes and colours. Others have barely changed at all. Palaeontologists have famously found fossils of horseshoe crabs (not crustaceans despite the name) dating back 450 million years, but they appear near-identical to their living counterparts. Masters of evolutionary procrastination, it could be said that no animal lineage has done less with more time than these.

At Sheppey, bivalves, gastropods and fish can all be found on the beaches as well, in the same exceptional three dimensions in the best nodules. Another speciality are the husks of the nina palm seeds, which are usually short and stocky, preserved in pyrite with the dark colour and texture not unlike a date.

The beaches are best accessed from the far ends, with car parks to be found at Minster-on-Sea and Warden Point. The cliffs are slumped and landfalls are common, so plenty of material winds up on the beach, with the light-coloured nodules your best bet to find something amazing, if you can keep an eye out for that little hint of black fossil to reveal an animal from a period in time few would ever even think about.

Beltinge

Specifically evolved to be resistant, and with so many examples found in each individual, teeth are common discoveries in the fossil world, and none are more immediately recognisable than those that have come from sharks. The classic shearing triangles or ragged spikes are pretty much unmistakable as coming from anything other than prehistoric jaws, and in no place in the UK can they be found more readily than Beltinge, just along from Herne Bay in Kent.

The low cliffs of Beltinge date mostly to the Eocene (55 million years ago), though the bases just about reach into the older Paleocene epoch. Most fossils originate from the rich beds around halfway up the cliff where, in a few spots, the transition between strata is quite distinct. The rock faces aren't the main focus here, however; instead you should be looking at sifting through material nearer the water.

Most of the specimens here are small (ranging from two to three centimetres for full teeth), not like the giant *megalodon* teeth we discussed earlier (see p.172). They're also usually completely free of any matrix, as their shape makes it quite easy for them to pop out of the rock naturally, so you can give your hammer a break and use your hands to fish them out. Just be careful as they're still sharp and can give a surprisingly nasty nip for a long-dead fish.

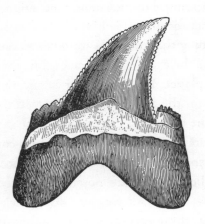

A shark tooth showing the triangular crown and rounded root

As well as their high preservation potential, other factors contribute to shark tooth abundance. Firstly, the frequency with which sharks lose teeth. We humans have two sets of teeth; starting with 'baby' teeth, replaced by 'adult' teeth. The scientific term for animals like us is diphyodont, and it's a trait common amongst mammals, but it's far from the norm in the greater animal kingdom.

Many reptile species (and probably dinosaurs as well) are polyphodonts, meaning that they have multiple replacement teeth over their lives. Crocodilians replace their teeth regularly, almost like shedding skin. But no group takes this concept to a greater extreme than the sharks. Sharks possess a feature called 'revolver dentition', meaning they have a queue of teeth backed up in their jaws, curled over in an assembly line. When one tooth falls, the next simply rolls over to replace it. This handy ability means sharks can play fast and loose with their teeth, not worrying about whether a few fall out whilst they aggressively take on prey.

Another thing that makes shark teeth so prevalent in the fossil record is the extreme expanse of time that sharks have been on the planet. You often hear it said that sharks are a relic left from the age of the dinosaurs; a line even used to promote the film *Jaws*. The truth is that sharks are even older than that; the earliest evidence of them comes from the Devonian period, 410 million years ago. That's more than 150 million years before the first dinosaurs and is older than trees of any kind.

Admittedly, these earliest fossils are tentative, so much so that Emma Bernard, curator of fish at the Natural History Museum, describes them as having come from 'the least shark-like shark'. And with the name *Doliodus problematicus*, it's clear palaeontologists have their reservations about this animal's true affinities, depending on how loosely you are willing to use the term 'shark'. From here, though, their lineage survived through the worst extinctions the earth has ever faced and they remain ocean masters today. The 55-million-year-old sharks of Beltinge suddenly appear as the youngsters of the family.

Even though identifying shark teeth is fairly easy, identifying exact species is trickier, as tooth shape is no guarantee of species clarification. Notoriously in the fossil world, a shark's tooth can vary enormously depending on where in the mouth it originated. Teeth on the upper jaw may be broad triangles, whereas the lower could be curved and thin. Two teeth initially presumed to be from different species could in theory be from the same individual animal.

As common as their teeth are, finding actual shark skeletons is extraordinarily rare. Sharks don't have mineralised skeletons; instead their bones are purely cartilage, which is far harder to fossilise, though deposition of calcium salts used to strengthen the cartilage can make preservation more possible. Fossil shark skeletons do exist, therefore, but are amongst the rarest of fossils out there. The same is true for stingrays, though their rounded crushing teeth palates can be found more readily.

Getting to Beltinge is relatively easy, thanks to the proximity of Herne Bay, though it is a long walk from there beyond the sea wall to the prime fossiling site. A small car park nearby at Reculver Drive (named for nearby Roman fortification ruins) can place you quickly in the heart of the site.

Shark teeth here are very abundant and scattered across the beach. Most are blackened and their smooth sheath makes them more reflective than the surrounding shingle and sand, meaning they're fairly easy to scout from the surface. Though shark teeth can be found in many places around the UK, Beltinge is really a cut above the rest.

Folkestone

The port of Dover is one of the busiest in the world; the gateway to France and mainland Europe sees more than ten million passengers pass through each year. One thing they can all see are the White Cliffs, a geological icon of Britain. There are fossils to be found in these cliffs, but for a palaeontologist, the more exciting cliffs lie a few miles to the west, near the town of Folkestone.

The cliffs here are lower than those at Dover, and the white chalk has been replaced for the most part by a dull grey. But the fossils here are anything but dull; there are many hidden gems waiting to be uncovered.

Still in the heyday of dinosaurs but after the age of those like *Iguanodon*, the rocks here date to the mid-Cretaceous (107 million years ago). The best fossils of Folkestone are from the marine community, in particular ammonites. This famous group was not entirely restricted to the Jurassic, but extended throughout a great span of geological time, first appearing in the Devonian before they became extinct along with the dinosaurs at the end of the Mesozoic, about forty million years after those at Folkestone.

What makes the many ammonites here so special is that they're preserved in such a way that their shells are iridescent, shining with multiple colours that change across the spectrum as you turn them in the light, as though splitting light with a prism, lending them a slight glint and pearlescent sheen, due to the presence of the mineral aragonite.

Aragonite is a form of calcium carbonate, just like the calcite we see in many other fossils. As with other mollusc species, then and now, ammonites had a layer of this aragonite inside their shells called the nacreous layer, often referred to as the 'mother of pearl' layer, and it's easy to see why. The orientation and alignment of the aragonite crystals are dictated by proteins produced by the animal and give it a structure that specially reflects the light. We see it in living animals too, such as the Pāua shells of New Zealand, and inside some oysters. Sometimes the aragonite can be layered around debris within the shell, slowly snowballing and ultimately resulting in the beautiful spheres we know as pearls, which can take years to grow to the sizes used in jewellery.

A common genus at Folkestone with this preservation is *Anahoplites*. This is what's known as an involute ammonite, which means the end of the shell (where the soft-body would once have been housed – the body chamber) slightly overlaps with the previous whorls, obscuring them from view. When there is no overlap and all parts of the spiral are totally visible, we call that 'evolute'.

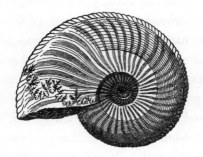

Anahoplites, an involute ammonite

Some ammonites that can be found here come in very strange shapes indeed. You may well find fragments of ammonites that don't seem to have much, if any, curve to them, making you wonder how they could have come from a tightly wound coil. But not all ammonites were the perfect spirals we imagine them to be; some could be uncoiled. They still retain that spiral structure in parts, but the coils might not even be touching, or they may be coiled only at the top before transitioning into a perfectly straight section of shell. One such example from Folkestone is the genus *Hamites*.

Ammonites and many other fossils can be easily extracted from the soft rocks and clays they're embedded in. Some can even be worked out of the matrix using only your fingers, though a field knife can be very handy for sites like this. A few other notable finds here include crustaceans, fish remains, and a few bits of marine reptile (though, as these rocks date from the Cretaceous, ichthyosaurs are substantially rarer by this point when compared to their Jurassic glory days).

The fossil location is easy enough to reach from the town, so long as you take the usual precautions of tidal timings. Just above the harbour is a small patch of sandy beach, but you don't need to walk far before you come across the clay and greensand cliffs that spill over the shore around Copt Point. The fossils come mostly from the central clay bands, with falls being quite regular. With such a diverse assemblage to be discovered, Folkestone is probably one of the richest Cretaceous fossil-hunting grounds not only in the south-east, but the entire UK, with falls being quite regular and fossils often washing into rockpools along the shore.

South-West England

Aust

Not many fossil localities are lucky enough to have distinct landmarks flagging their positions as prominently as the cliffs of Aust. Right on the banks of the River Severn, this site is unmissable thanks to the gigantic bridge erupting directly from it. Aust, a gateway to the south-west, is bisected by the Old Severn Bridge (not the newer and bluer 'Prince of Wales Bridge', but rather, the original white suspension bridge opened in 1966).

The 40-metre cliffs are predominantly red in colour, before a rather sudden transformation to grey and black near the top. This colour change in the cliff marks the layer where the fossils are most densely packed, the Aust Bone Bed, dating to the very end of the Triassic (208 million years ago). It's impossible to inspect the cliffs directly, but frequent falls mean there are always plenty of fossils on the beach.

Fossil hunting is a mysterious lucky dip at the best of times, and there are few places where this is more true than at Aust. The chunks of bone bed littering the shore are packed full of fossils; small and often shiny black structures scattered in the blue and grey matrix. The fossils at Aust were formed in a cave system, similar to those seen in South Wales. Just like caves today, the tide washes in material from the seas, collecting it all together in one place; this includes the remains of animals. Having been smashed around by the waves before they were even entombed in rock, the fossils here are, frankly, a mess.

Unfortunately, the Aust fossils can be a case of quantity over quality. Owing to the site's history at the mercy of the sea's violent waves, most complex fossils are fragmented beyond recognition. 'Long bones' are usually broken, making it surprisingly difficult to distinguish between even wildly different bone types, to the point where it's difficult to deduce a rib from a tibia without careful examination.

None of this is to say that spectacular fossils don't still emerge from the rock here; it's just that most of them are small. Teeth are some of the most common and can be perfectly preserved. Some are conical, with strong ribbing on the sides. These are the teeth of ichthyosaurs and are quite regularly found here. Another distinctive find are the small three-peaked teeth of a group of sharks called hybodonts.

Teeth aren't the best shark fossils you can hope to find here, though, as hybodonts have one feature that is missing from modern sharks. These are long black bones, ranging in size from just a few centimetres to almost half a metre, all of them showing clear and deep grooves running parallel along their length. If you find one complete enough, you might even find it tapering to a point, and triangular spikes protruding from the flattest edge.

On first sight, it could be mistaken for a jaw, but this is not the case. The clue is in the tapering – this is a spike. A long spine protruded from the top of these hybodont sharks, just in front of the dorsal fin. Teeth not enough, these Mesozoic sharks had extra weaponry. Some even had smaller versions above their eyes, like bull horns.

The reason for these spikes is nothing to do with catching prey, though, but rather, quite the opposite. We're used to sharks being apex predators, but to the giant marine reptiles of the Mesozoic, sharks were just like any other fish in the sea, suitable prey for hungry monsters. These spines were added protection to avoid ending up on the menu.

Hybodonts weren't the only prehistoric predatory fish to have bizarre extra features, making our modern species almost mundane in comparison. The most famous are the Devonian *Stethacanthus* with an ironing-board-like structure on top of the dorsal fin, and *Heliocoprion* of the Permian, which had a whorl of teeth like an ammonite shell loaded in its jaw. The exact purposes of these bizarre structures are currently unknown. We cannot use the word 'shark' for either of these, as they in fact belong to a very closely related group, though they effectively inhabit the same environmental niche.

What Aust is known for above all else are fossils that at first defy interpretation. For every clear bone, scale or tooth fossil you see in the rock, there will likely be a few amorphous black blobs in there too. The same colour as the others, these are fossils and not just geological features in the rock. More than any other location in the UK, Aust has an abundance of coprolites.

Coprolite is the scientific name given to fossilised dung. After all, it stands to reason that, with everything else that can become fossilised, so too can animal waste. Even though they can come from a diverse range of animals, coprolites typically aren't exciting fossils to look at, although some are impressively large (most are around two centimetres in diameter, but examples can be found that are closer in size to cannonballs). To a scientist, though, coprolites can be used to reveal details of past animal diets.

When CT-scanned, it is revealed that fish scales are a common component of these coprolites, and can also be found loose in the rock matrix. Easy to spot as small and shiny black flecks in the rock, the shape and distinct grooves of the scales can identify their fish owners. In the case of many Aust scales, this appears to have been largely the genus *Gyrolepis*. A recent study by Emily Green of the University of Lincoln revealed that this unfortunate fish was a top menu choice for many predators of the area.

Aust is an interesting site, as any visitor is more or less guaranteed to come away with a high abundance of fossils, though they'll be a jumbled assortment at best.

The tide is a huge factor here. It's a five- to ten-minute walk onto the beach site from Passage Road and you don't want to get caught out. This is even more vital to bear in mind if you venture under the bridge to the other side (though it isn't as fossiliferous as the near side). Aust is certainly well worth a visit, however, even if the finds are mostly a load of coprolite.

Avon Gorge

Many UK cities have spots of geological intrigue hidden within them, but few are as overtly on display as those that run through the city of Bristol. Sculpting the landscape, the Avon Gorge extends for a mile and a half, with walls more than three hundred feet tall, dividing Clifton and the city to the east, and Leigh Woods and suburbs to the west. The region owes its most iconic manmade landmark to this natural feature: the Clifton Suspension Bridge, spanning the 214-metre width of the gorge, as Isambard Kingdom Brunel's most recognisable design.

Looking at the geology specifically, the rock is mostly Carboniferous limestone, though Devonian and Triassic strata are also exposed. Much of the limestone has undergone a process known as dolomitization (essentially increasing the concentration of magnesium in the rock), giving some layers a distinctive dark red colouration. Other natural features include 'Bristol Diamonds', not actual diamonds but large quartz geodes common around the gorge.

Fossils are common, although these are locked in the solid walls of the gorge and are therefore not collectable. Brachiopod shell fragments are common, as are collections of rugose corals and crinoid ossicles, both of which can be concentrated in thin bands. There are relatively few fossils visible from ground level, but the gorge is very popular with climbing groups, and if you're adventurous enough to scale the walls with one of these professional groups, then you'll no doubt find others preserved at height.

One odd quirk of geology here is a bizarre result of both natural and human activity. Near the suspension bridge, a short section of rock is exposed, sloping downwards towards a path. A long time ago, presumably predating the bridge, locals realised it was the perfect slope to act as a slide. The only issue was that the rock surface was coarse and not the most comfortable ride, but generations of Bristolians had the solution. Despite the discomfort, more and more continued to slide, each slowly eroding and smoothing it out to the point that today it shines, polished to the point of being reflective.

The Avon Gorge may be more prominent, but no fossil discovery here matched one made in a quarry just a short walk away. In the 1820s, Bristol was growing, and it would soon become one of the very first places in the world to construct a zoo. At a quarry near the gorge, miners gathered construction materials. Whilst excavating, one noticed white structures in the red rock that looked distinctly like bones. Together, the founder of the project, Henry Riley, and the curator of what we now call the Bristol Museum, Samuel Stutchbury, set about identifying them. They quickly decided that they must have belonged to some ancient crocodile. One of the key fossils was that of a lower jaw lined with teeth, each embedded in a socket. From this the animal was given a name, *Thecodontosaurus*, 'socket-toothed lizard'.

Riley and Stutchbury were wrong. What they'd unknowingly just found was Bristol's very own dinosaur, the fourth to be discovered and a full fourteen years before the invention of the word 'dinosaur', it wouldn't be identified as such until years later.

Today, our picture of the Bristol dinosaur, nicknamed Theco, is far clearer. Theco was a small omnivore, standing on two legs a little more than half a metre high and with a length of one and a half metres, comparable in size to something like a sheep. An early dinosaur in more than one sense, Theco came from the Triassic, the first dinosaur to ever have been found from this geological period.

Though small in stature, Theco's family had a big future. *Thecodontosaurus* was an early relative of the sauropod dinosaurs, a group which contained giants like *Diplodocus*, *Brachiosaurus* and *Cetiosaurus*, though, owing to the fact that Britain was then a series of tropical islands, the initial growth of this group was limited by resources.

After many questionable reconstructions over the years, a life-sized model of Theco was constructed in 2013 by palaeoartist Bob Nichols (the same artist behind Cardiff's *Dracoraptor*), and this model now stands proudly in the dinosaur gallery of the Bristol Museum & Art Gallery.

As for the quarry itself, excavation activities ended long ago. Today, as with so many other locations, houses have been built on the former site, leaving much of it hidden, though one section remains exposed. More or less completely hidden unless you know it's there, a quiet backstreet alleyway of stairs runs through a residential area on the borders of the Clifton and Durdham Downs. Called Quarry Steps, here you can stand and look over at a single surviving rock face of the old mining activity. There are no signs to tell you of the scientific significance, so many are unaware of this old dinosaur discovery site on their doorstep.

The rock is now inaccessible, so today exists as a visual curiosity rather than an active fossil-hunting site. The discovery of a dinosaur barely paused the activity of the quarry as a whole, and the rock mined from here continued to be used to fuel the growth of the city. As intended, some went on to build the outer walls of Bristol Zoo Gardens, meaning that there's every chance fragmented bits of dinosaur missed by workers may have ended up being used. Visitors to the zoo would do well to keep a close eye out for any traces of this hidden animal attraction.

Watchet

Ammonites are some of the most commonly found and sought-after fossils in the UK. With their pretty, distinctive whorls, they are some of the most iconic fossils of all, but few are familiar with those that can be found around Watchet in Somerset.

The predominantly dark mudstone cliffs here preserve the first major transition within the Mesozoic, from the Triassic to the Jurassic. Most fossils come from near the tops of these cliffs, around 201 million years ago, and that familiar Blue Lias group, a particularly fossil-rich layer of blue-hued limestone and shale.

A major species here is *Psiloceras planorbis*, interesting for a number of reasons, such as the fact that it possesses what is, by ammonite standards, an exceptionally smooth shell. There's no distinct ribbing or large suture lines visible (the walls of the chambers in the shell which can often be seen as fuzzy lines on the external surface), but instead a simple, gentle spiral. *P. planorbis* is also a great zone fossil, used for dating the specific rock layers in the cliffs.

This feature was famously used by William Smith, a geologist who collected several of these ammonites from Watchet. Combined with his study of other fossils (like the pound stones of Cross Hands Quarry – see p.148), he began to correlate units of rock and to research where the same strata reappeared across the country. Using this data, he produced the world's first national-scale geological map, charting the bedrock of England and Wales in 1815.

What makes the Watchet Psiloceras *planorbis* special is how they're preserved. They are not three-dimensional casts or calcite structures like those we're used to. Rather, these ammonites have been crushed completely flat, and have a remarkable iridescence, owing to the presence of aragonite in their shells. Similarly iridescent ammonites can be seen in Folkestone (see p.189), but those at Watchet are in a league of their own, with rainbow colours quite unlike anything you'll see elsewhere. They aren't the only ones either, as another, rarer species, *Caloceras johnstoni*, is also found similarly preserved as a flattened rainbow, easy to tell apart from *Psiloceras* as it has ribbing on the shell spiral.

The aragonite within these shells means that, when they are crushed by the weight of the overlying rock, the minerals within the ammonite fossils align to create even more vivid rainbow colourations, with the exact spectral array dependent partly on the original thickness of the shell. Though the vivid multicolour examples do happen, you're most likely to find them in deep reds, whilst others will have a whiter hue.

These fossils are surprisingly common if you know how to spot them. Whilst they can be found pre-exposed on the surface of the rocks on the beach, you're more likely to find them complete if you look out for flat stones with small slivers of colour or white along their edges. These indicate that the rocks may well have ammonites inside them and should be quite easy to split open. Even if you see nothing around the edges, these flat shales are well worth investigating.

Plenty of other fossils can be found at Watchet, with exceptionally large ammonites (in the more traditional three-dimensional preservation) and marine reptile material popping up in nodules along the beach. It's certainly a good idea to carefully check the rounded boulders as well as the flatter shales.

There are several similar locations along this part of the Somerset coast to have these same fossiliferous beds, where you can find not only amazing fossils but great geology as well. Standing out in particular is one excellent section of clearly folded rock halfway along the beach, beautifully demonstrating features straight out of a structural geology textbook. The flat beds of rock that make up the shore are themselves quite something, even if they are less fossiliferous than the cliff debris. Tracking along the sea line, they form dramatic platforms and shallow amphitheatres of stone.

The stretches from Watchet to Blue Anchor can be easily accessed from the town of Watchet itself, walking straight down onto the beach near the harbour. Other places towards Quantoxhead are more remote but parking can still be found at nearby Kilve to give you beach access, with public transport options limited.

Cheddar Gorge

The south-west is home to one of the most magnificent and breathtaking geological structures in Britain, but all that is utterly overshadowed in fame by a dairy product that happens to be produced near it. I am of course referring to Cheddar Gorge.

A name synonymous with cheese, it can surprise some to learn that the town of Cheddar is quite literally situated under a geological colossus, one with limestone walls that are more than one hundred and thirty metres in height and run for a length of three miles. The gorge is worth a visit purely for the wonder of scenic surroundings, but there is palaeontological heritage here too. Before we discuss that, however, it is necessary to give a brief summary of just how the UK's largest gorge formed in the first place.

As with almost all such features, Cheddar Gorge started out small, as no more than a seasonal stream slowly eroding its way through the underlying rock. This gradual process was set off explosively by glacial activity during the Ice Age, during which fast-flowing meltwater carved rapidly through the soft Carboniferous limestone. Though it may look as though it's been there for ever, the gorge is quite a recent development, all of this taking place within the past million years, during the Pleistocene epoch.

When the water table sat below the surface, the water would continue to flow through the permeable rocks beneath, an activity invisible from ground level. These erosive forces carved a complex system of caves in the area, plenty of which are still open today (though many remain flooded and inaccessible, save for adventurous professionals with scuba gear and years of training). They also house the Cheddar Yeo, which is the largest underground river system in the country. These caves play an important role in the area's other export of repute too, as the cheese made here is aged within the caves as a traditional part of the process.

Today, with no glacial meltwater to supercharge it, the erosion of the gorge has slowed considerably, making it much more of a static geological system than it had once been. The stream too has been replaced by a man-made river of asphalt road.

The exposure of all that limestone makes fossils common, although, just as with the Avon Gorge, the fact that they are, for the most part, locked in those towering walls means they can't be collected. That said, they can still be spotted in the rocks all over the area, showing a community of Carboniferous marine fossils, with brachiopods and rugose corals the most common finds.

Coral remains aren't the only fossils here, even if the word 'fossils' should perhaps not be used for these other finds. Many of the discoveries here tread a fine line between prehistory and history, the realm where palaeontology and archaeology meet.

Thousands of years ago, wild animals used the caves here for shelter, and some were taken there after being hunted. Most prominently, up until only a few hundred years ago, the UK was home to wolves, and their remains, and those of their unfortunate prey, still litter many of the caves around the country.

Some other species found at Cheddar Gorge are far more familiar to us, with the list of ancient animal remains including the species *Homo sapiens*.

Of all the prehistoric materials found in the gorge, none have been more extensively studied than those of 'Cheddar Man'. Discovered in Gough's Cave at the start of the twentieth century, these bones are dated to about 9,100 years ago. Though far from the oldest human remains in the country (a title held by a jawbone from Kent's Cavern in Torquay – more than four times as old, dated to about 42,000 years ago), this specimen is the oldest complete skeleton ever found in Britain.

The fact that the skeleton was so complete has naturally warranted a great deal of interest in Cheddar Man, and years of research have revealed much about the life behind the bones. We know that it was indeed a male human, with dark skin and hair, and that he likely had blue eyes. Such specific details can be predicted thanks to Cheddar Man being so palaeontologically recent that DNA can be extracted from the bones; a heritage study was carried out, tracking down some of the man's descendants. Remarkably, these relatives were local; almost ten thousand years on, they remained in Somerset.

Caves are important sites in recent palaeontology, with some of the most remarkable discoveries of the time being made by spelunkers (another term for cavers) on expeditions in the mysterious underground layers many might fear to tread. Areas around the south-west, such as the Mendip Hills, are rich in skeletal remains, many of which are now hidden away in privately owned caving museums. Remarkable specimens in such collections include mammoth tusks and limb bones, the skulls of wolves, deer and all kinds of mammals. One particularly notable specimen is an ancient human skull with a very clear chunk missing from the top, a chunk matching perfectly with the size and shape you'd expect from an axe blow.

Caves are a rich resource for the science of palaeontology, but it should go without saying how extremely specialist it is to explore them. Cave fossil hunting is not like any of the other experiences discussed in this book. It requires expertise and a great deal of safety precautions, and should not be attempted unless done correctly with the guidance of trained professionals.

A top tourist attraction of the region, Cheddar Gorge is easy to access, with regular buses journeying in from the surrounding area and plentiful parking for drivers, though it should be noted that any cars parking in the gorge itself do so with the understanding that there is a risk of potential damage from falling rocks.

There is much more in the way of natural history than people first expect when hearing the word 'Cheddar'. Oh, and rumour has it there is also cheese.

Valley of the Rocks

Few places are more perfectly named for their geological prestige than the Valley of the Rocks, found near the Exmoor coast of North Devon. More than a fitting name, the dramatic rise of the jagged rock faces surely make this one of the most beautiful fossil-collecting spots. This is not merely just a personal opinion, but one shared by the multitude of poets and artists to have drawn inspiration from the striking landscape, including William Wordsworth and Samuel Taylor Coleridge.

The rocks in question are dated to 393 million years ago, placing them in the Devonian period, making them far older than any rocks we've encountered in the south so far, but perhaps this isn't at all surprising; there is nothing coincidental about finding Devonian rocks in the county of Devon, as the time period is named after the county.

It was not these grey fossiliferous shales of the valley that inspire the name, but rather, the vast collection of strata known as the 'Old Red Sandstone'. This geological unit is found in huge deposits across Europe and North America, and it was first studied in detail here in Devon. There are sections of that sandstone nearby, but, being a remnant of the barren Devonian landmass, before many plants or animals had managed to evolve to live out of the seas, there are no fossils to be found within them.

The large-scale scenery may be what artists came to admire, but palaeontologists should instead focus on the scree that surrounds them.

Some of the slates show a regular pattern on their surface, looking almost as though small chunks of a tight-meshed fishnet has embedded into them, the lines creating little rectangular windows with rounded edges. If enough is preserved, you can note the fact that the lines don't run perfectly straight, but fan out slightly, as if arcing from a central point. Originating in the Devonian seas, these are too early to be the impressions of reptile scales or even plant patterns as we've seen before. They belong to a form of colonial marine invertebrates known as bryozoans.

Despite being around for 480 million years and remaining highly diverse and widespread today (almost 6,000 species across seven continents), they aren't a particularly well-known group of organisms. Much like graptolites, bryozoans are an aggregation of individuals (each known as a zooid) living together, filtering food from the water with the hair-like cilia on their tentacles beating to produce a current of water to drive food particles towards the mouth. Bryozoans do not float through the seas but are fixed in one place in their adult form, encrusting onto a stationary surface like a rock, and staying there for ever. In this respect, they're more like corals. But bryozoans aren't closely related to either; surprisingly, they are in fact more closely related to brachiopods and worms.

The most common species that can be found in the Valley of the Rocks is *Fenestella antiqua*, appropriately meaning 'little old window', perfectly describing how the fossils appear on the rocks. It was into these 'windows' that the soft-bodied zooid would protrude in life, with the 'mesh' being the skeleton, holding the colony together and adding structural strength to the animal.

You may also find these specimens displaying the reverse of what I've described, these being the cast moulds of the fossil. In these fossils, rather than a pitted 'mesh net' the slate will have a knobbly texture, where the 'windows' dome out from the surface, still in those distinctly regular sizes and spacings.

Alongside these bryozoans are all the usual suspects of Devonian marine fauna: brachiopods and bivalves are common as ever, and crinoids too are surprisingly prevalent (often of the genus *Hexacrinites*).

The Valley of the Rocks is a popular location for artists and scientists alike, and is suitably accessible, the main car park backing directly onto one of the prime fossil-bearing areas. There's even a café directly on the site.

On top of the fossils, you will no doubt notice the living residents as well, the valley currently being home to a thriving population of feral goats. If you feel your blood pressure isn't quite high enough, then it might be worth taking some time to watch these four-legged residents flaunt all the codes of practice for field work by traversing the near-vertical rock faces with ease, utterly indifferent to the feats of balance they're accomplishing on their journeys to the good grass for lunch.

Lizard Point

Reaching out towards the Atlantic, the long country roads of Cornwall come to a halt at the westernmost tip of mainland Britain, the fittingly named Land's End. Having journeyed down nearly the entirety of the country we have not yet discussed the absolute pinnacle, must-see location of UK palaeontology and, pleasing though it would be in a narrative sense, that place is not Land's End. In fact, the deeper you head into Cornwall, the rarer the chances to find fossils seem to be, due to a general lack of fossil-bearing exposures. But don't let the lack of fossils lead you to believe there's no geological interest here.

Cornwall has quite a unique geology, different from pretty much the whole of the rest of England. The igneous landscape here would seem more at home in Scotland than the south-west. It even possesses its own unique vocabulary, with the verb 'fossicking' used to describe fossil hunting, a term used only here and apparently Australia and New Zealand (assuming my Aussie and Kiwi colleagues aren't just pulling my leg).

No more so is the dramatic nature of Cornwall's geology preserved than around Lizard Point. The name doesn't come from the discovery of ancient or modern lizards (though all three British-native lizards can be found here); instead it comes from the old Cornish word 'Lezou', meaning headland.

The Lizard is an example of an ophiolite, formed as a result of plate tectonics. Continental plates are those which form the land masses of the earth, rising higher as a result of their lower density composition than oceanic plates, which form the ocean floors. When the two different plates collide, the oceanic plate is forced under the continental and this can be a common cause of earthquakes and volcanic eruptions. An ophiolite like Lizard is, in effect, like the reverse of this. This is a place where oceanic crustal rock has been shoved up to sit on top of the continental. The reason the geology here is so different is because it's unlike any other crustal section in the UK. This is a mass of oceanic rock masquerading as regular land.

Much of the bedrock of the Lizard is made up of peridotite, one of the most common rock types on the planet, though its name is not well known, as it is rarely visible, the majority of it contained within the upper mantle, deep within the earth. As a rock, it is fairly plain, mostly black in colour, the most eye-catching feature being inclusions of bright green crystals.

These crystals are of the mineral olivine, which are very common within the earth and are regularly found in igneous rocks. Due to their appealing colour, upon finding a loose boulder, this might be a tempting feature to collect in order to satisfy your inner mineralogist, but make sure to do so with care. Taking a hammer to an igneous rock is very different from the regular sedimentary ones. Igneous rocks are crystalline and far denser, leading to issues with dangerous rock splintering.

Spanning a few square miles, it's hard to narrow down the Lizard to any one particular location to best view its features. As is often the case in earth sciences, where it can be seen most readily remains where the rock is naturally exposed at the coast.

At nearby Mullion Island, you can see another basalt geological feature, though these are quite unlike those seen at the Giant's Causeway (see p.58). Here, instead of geometric hexagons, the basalt is found in rounded, dome-like shapes, known in geology as 'pillow lava'.

Although Cornwall may not be the best place in the UK for fossil hunting, the unique display of geology makes it fascinating. But, if there is a dearth of fossils here, then it is more than made up for by the immense concentration of them only a few miles away, as not far along the south coast lies by far the richest area for fossils in the country.

Jurassic Coast

Jurassic Coast – West

The beaches of Lyme Regis and Charmouth are a phenomenal source of fossils, but before we go into site specifics, we must first talk about the wider region they are a part of, the Jurassic Coast. This is an area so rich in fossils that, along with the neighbouring Isle of Wight, it warrants an independent chapter. These locations combine a perfect storm of conditions to form fossils; that is, a shallow marine environment swarming with life, with a modern coastline that ensures maximum exposure of the fossil-bearing rocks.

The Jurassic Coast extends for 95 miles, with fossil localities of that age stretching from Axmouth to the Isle of Purbeck, and is frequently ranked among the best places to find fossils in the world, not just the UK. The coast is not a singular site, but a collection of them. Here, moving west to east, we'll explore a few in more detail, each of which has revealed amazing fossils. Together, they build up a detailed picture of Mesozoic Britain.

Most celebrated of all is the very first stop, Lyme Regis and Charmouth, right on the border of Devon. One of the main reasons it's so well known is due to it being the home of the most famous and inspirational fossil hunter of all time, Mary Anning.

During the first half of the 1800s, these beaches were Anning's domain, where she excavated an astonishing abundance of remains from the limestone and shale sequence called the Blue Lias. The impact Anning had on the early science of palaeontology cannot be overstated, and her finds completely transformed our views of the ancient world. Sadly, as she was a woman in Georgian England, her contributions were not recognised enough during her lifetime, and it wasn't until well after her death that people began to understand and truly appreciate her as one of science's great pioneers.

The more you learn about her, the more interesting she gets: Anning survived a lightning strike, potentially inspired the tongue-twister 'She sells seashells on the seashore', and drew some of the most extraordinary scientific illustrations ever made. Anning uncovered fossilised cephalopods with their black-ink sacks so well preserved that she was able to use the ink to make sketches of some of her ichthyosaur discoveries.

The majority of UK ichthyosaurs, including the most frequent find here, *Ichthyosaurus communis*, would grow no larger than around three metres, though some could grow much larger. *Opthalmosaurus*, for instance, could reach six metres, and topping the Jurassic charts at more than eleven metres is the monstrous *Temnodontosaurus*.

The *Temnodontosaurus* would have been an apex predator of the Jurassic seas, hunting down other marine reptiles. If you find what appear to be regular ichthyosaur bones but far larger, the chances are that they belong to one of these beasts. And if you are lucky enough to find substantial remains, don't expect to get them out whole, as they can literally weigh tonnes. Forget the dinosaurs; this giant ichthyosaur may well have been the largest predator Britain has ever known.

Marine reptiles weren't alone in the seas, and fossils of fish can also be found at Lyme Regis. One of the most impressive genera is *Dapedium*. This round-bodied fish can grow to more than forty centimetres in length, and its thick, bony scales have made it more likely a candidate for fossilisation than some others. These scales are the most commonly found fossils of *Dapedium*, appearing as flattened, diamond-shaped patterns of highly reflective black rock. *Dapedium*'s mouth was equipped with powerful jaws and teeth to aid it in crushing hard-shelled food items like brachiopods and ammonites.

There are more than just marine life fossils to be found here, though. In the winter of 1828, Mary Anning uncovered a series of very fragile bones, quite different from the usual ichthyosaurs that can be discovered in this area. This bizarre animal was soon identified as a pterosaur, the flying reptiles of the Mesozoic (spanning almost the entire era with a duration from 230 to 66 million years ago), which, it is vital to stress, are *not* dinosaurs. This was the first pterosaur to be found outside of Germany, the only place they had previously been found. Unlike the slender heads of the German species, however, this pterosaur was quite stocky, with slender but sharp teeth for catching prey. It was given the name *Dimorphodon* and is one of the better-known pterosaurs in palaeontology today.

Pterosaur bones are rare in any location due to their delicate nature, meaning they're more readily lost or destroyed prior to fossilisation. This delicate nature would have been utterly necessary, however: as with any flying animal, pterosaurs needed to be as lightweight as possible. Their bones are not only small but also hollow, another weight-shedding tactic.

The wing structure of these animals is particularly peculiar. They don't use feathers like a bird, but skin, like a bat. Whereas a bat extends this skin across elongated fingers of their hands, the whole final stretch of a pterosaur wing is just their third finger, which has been elongated to ludicrous proportions. The membrane then connects the tip of this bizarre finger to their ankle to create the wing surface.

Dimorphodon was a relatively small pterosaur with a wingspan of one and a half metres, comparable to a modern buzzard in size. The teeth show that it was a carnivore, likely surviving on small prey such as insects or fish. Unlike some of its larger relatives such as the famous crested *Pteranodon* of North America (the animal most of us envisage when thinking of pterosaurs), *Dimorphodon* also had a long bony tail, which was a feature common in earlier members of this group.

Not be left out, the famous reptiles of the land also make an appearance. In 2000, fossil hunter David Sole (not the former Scotland rugby captain) was inspecting a 60-centimetre slab of limestone embedded in the rocky sand of Charmouth Beach that turned out to be the discovery of a lifetime. Showing the dedication such finds can take, it was months before all the material was extracted. Once prepared, the limestone revealed a collection of black fossils all from a single 3.1-metre-long individual animal. At the time of writing, this is the most complete dinosaur skeleton ever discovered in Britain.

The dinosaur was a Jurassic herbivore called *Scelidosaurus*. It wasn't exactly a giant, but it was far from small, and what it may have lacked in size, it more than made up for in defence. *Scelidosaurus* was covered in armour plating, with hardened short spikes (scutes) scattered all over the skeleton, from the head to the tip of the tail.

Scelidosaurus was an early member of an evolutionary pathway that would later result in some famous dinosaur types, including the plated *Stegosaurus* and armoured ankylosaurs.

The complete remains of David Sole's discovery are on display in the Bristol Museum & Art Gallery, alongside other partial remains of juveniles also found at Charmouth.

Before moving on, there is one last incredible thing to mention of the *Scelidosaurus* specimens of Charmouth. Amongst the regular remains of armoured skeleton have been found, amazingly, preserved skin impressions. This allows us to say for certain that around the scutes was scaly skin similar to that of modern reptiles. Skin is exceptionally rare and just about one of the most fragile fossils out there.

Preserved as dark material in association with the fossils, skin can be exceptionally useful to scientists, best demonstrated in marine reptiles. Until specimens were found with a skin outline preserved, nobody knew the body shape of an ichthyosaur; the dorsal fin and tail fluke not being represented by the skeleton, and therefore not known. Recent research of pigment structures in the preserved skin have even shown evidence of countershading (dark on top and light underneath) in marine reptile bodies, a camouflage technique seen today in many marine animals, such as the great white shark.

Marine invertebrates are commonly found here, and none more famous than the local ammonites, a proud symbol of the area. These come in a wide variety of sizes, with some of the largest forming the spectacular 'Ammonite Pavement' of Lyme Regis, an area on the western shores where countless examples of them are entombed in the limestone under your feet on the shore. Some of these can measure up to seventy centimetres in diameter with the most common genus being *Coroniceras*.

Towards the Charmouth side there is the potential to find some incredible ammonites in the blackened shales, with some of the most prized being the heavily ribbed *Asteroceras* and *Promicroceras*, which can be found preserved in translucent calcite, and which look stunning with the matrix removed. In the best-preserved specimens their shells look as if decorated with feathery patterns. These are the suture lines of the shells, the more complex shapes lending them a stronger structure.

A common feature of the Black Ven cliffs of Charmouth are the 'golden ammonites', specimens preserved in iron pyrite (fool's gold). These ammonites are typically small, only one or two centimetres in diameter, and are highly variable in find frequency. On some days you can find hundreds of them have fallen from the cliffs, and on other days find barely any. Most are of the evolute and ribbed *Echioceras*, but you can also find examples of the flatter and involute *Oxynoticeras*. The common ending of 'ceras' in most ammonites means 'horn'.

Being such a well-known locality does come at a cost, as the beaches of Lyme Regis and Charmouth are frequently described as 'over-collected'. This is especially true in the summer months, when tourists from around the world flock here to try their hands at collecting. Bearing this in mind, it is well worth considering visiting these stretches on a day of less-than-ideal weather, as it might bring you more joy in the fossil department (bearing in mind to always be careful of the crumbling cliffs, of course).

However, even with the over-collection this is a spectacular area to find fossils – more so than it is possible to cover in one chapter alone. Belemnites can be found in stunning abundance here, as can crinoids, which can be found complete in thin sheets of pyrite. You will never leave a trip to the Jurassic coast without having seen great fossils, and there are plenty of museums in the area where you can see some of the most staggering finds and connect with the natural history and scientific heritage of the world's most famous fossil-hunting locality.

Jurassic Coast – East

Most of the celebrated sites of the Jurassic Coast are west of Weymouth, but the fossil-bearing cliffs reach to the east as well. One of the first sites you can discover on this side of the Isle of Portland is Osmington Mills.

At Osmington you'll mostly come across extensive bivalve collections, including the ever-present *Gryphaea* (the curved oyster-like shell fossils nicknamed 'devil's toenails' first seen on p.125). The limestone boulders emanating from the cliffs here are so densely populated with marine shells that you're guaranteed to find some great specimens. The bobbly-shelled clam *Myophorella* is one of the most common, especially towards the eastern edge. Typically preserved in dark colours, you might even catch them from a glint in a slightly reflective surface, as they are commonly preserved in iron pyrite (like fool's gold). But with great patience, this rock has also yielded far more impressive finds.

Over the course of nearly a decade, local café owner Kevan Sheehan painstakingly excavated a true monster from the beach as it slowly weathered from the cliffs. When prepared and put together, these bones assembled an incredible 2.1-metre-long skull, complete with a strong jaw containing huge conical teeth that would have belonged to a truly enormous predator. This is the Weymouth Bay pliosaur, *Pliosaurus kevani*, which you can find in the Dorchester County Museum. Estimated to have potentially reached twelve metres in length, this is the animal challenging to take *Temnodontosaurus'* crown as Britain's largest predator, though this will remain speculative unless a full skeleton is found.

Pliosaurs are actually highly specialised plesiosaurs, part of the same animal order. As such, they share many features, their bodies and paddles looking much the same. Where they differ is at the front; plesiosaurs are known for their long necks and small heads, whereas pliosaurs are much stockier and more heavily built. They have short necks and huge skulls, specialised for hunting other large marine reptiles.

The teeth of pliosaurs are perhaps their most recognisable features, as each one is a similar shape and size to that of a gently curved banana, albeit one with a very pointed and ridged cap. Several species are known from the UK, with two even discovered in the same clay pit in Westbury. The latter of these, *Pliosaurus carpenteri*, is the most complete pliosaur ever found in the country, full enough to have a full-sized eight-metre reconstruction made. Nicknamed 'Doris', this model can now be found hanging from the ceiling of Bristol Museum.

Another popular member of the group is *Liopleurodon*, made famous by the *Walking with Dinosaurs* TV series, which was discovered in the Oxford Clay near Peterborough. In life this species would have been much smaller than was depicted on screen, though being comparable to a basking shark at six metres in length, it was hardly small. That said, hugely overestimating the size of marine reptiles is a popular trope in pop culture (look no further than the mosasaur, which is at least three-times too big in *Jurassic World*).

Continuing east of Osmington, you reach Ringstead Bay and the intriguingly named 'Burning Cliff'. Named with good reason, the black shales here are rich in the chemical compound kerogen, and were you to put a lighter to some of them, they may actually combust. If left to burn long enough, the shale can turn a yellow or red colour thanks to the sulphur content in the rock. To state the obvious, though, just because an object *can* burn doesn't mean it should be done. You don't want to risk injury or become an accidental arsonist because of a field chemistry experiment.

Beyond this interesting feature, there are plenty of Jurassic fossils in these rocks, including another chance to bring up some very small but hugely diverse and important invertebrates, the gastropods.

A question that invariably arises when thinking of gastropods is how to tell them apart from those more famous spiral fossils, the ammonites. The most pronounced differences are seen when you consider what's usually missing from fossils: the soft-bodies. Ammonites are cephalopods, like squid, and similarly to them, they have tentacles and large eyes surrounding beak-like mouth parts. Snails are also molluscs, but a very different group, having one large fleshy 'foot', and smaller eyes mounted on stalks. This reflects their modes of life; one free-swimming and the other moving along the floor through waves of muscular contractions of its foot.

Inside the shell is also very different. Ammonites contain their entire body in one single chamber, the large end section, called the body chamber. The remainder are filled with gases and fluids to aid in buoyancy and swimming. Snails, in contrast, take up the entire shell as one continued chamber. Contrary to what is seen in cartoons, the shell is an integral part of the snail, housing their internal organs. This inability to separate the animal from its shell home is common across snails and ammonites.

Making things more complicated, though, there is a third group, the nautiloids. A spiral-shelled cephalopod with tentacles, moving by jet propulsion, this group sounds remarkably similar to ammonites. One big difference is that they're still alive today. The nautilus, found in the seas of the Indo-Pacific, is considered the closest living approximation we have to what an ammonite could have looked like, though there remain many key differences.

The most obvious is that ammonites became extinct 66 million years ago, so if you find a similar spiral cephalopod in younger rocks, it's a nautilus. But when it comes to Jurassic rocks like those here, you need to compare their anatomy.

All the nautiloids here have smooth shells, whereas ammonites often have clear ribbing, giving them a bumpy look and feel. However, this isn't universal, as ammonites can be smooth too. Internal structures are more telling. We've seen ammonites with intricate, feathery suture lines, but in nautiloids, they are all uniformly simple, following the same elegant curve.

Another feature can only be seen in the very best specimens. Both have a tube connecting the chambers inside the shell, the siphuncle. In ammonites it runs close to the outer edge of the shell, but in nautiloids it runs directly through the middle of each chamber wall. This is probably the most diagnostic feature to find, though the odds of finding a specimen well enough preserved to show it are low.

Beyond Ringstead Bay, the cliffs are steeper and not as accessible for fossil collecting. However, as we continue down this extremely rich coastline, we come across geological structures just as spectacular, which are explored in the next section.

The end of the Jurassic Coast is marked by the Isle of Purbeck, another misnomer, as it is connected to the mainland, and is in fact just a headland sticking into the English Channel near Poole Harbour. The area is popular with tourists for seaside towns like Swanage, natural beauty spots like the moorland nature reserves, and the historically impressive ruins of Corfe Castle.

For our interests, though, the Isle of Purbeck is the last hurrah in the incredible Mesozoic fossil extravaganza before the rocks give way to the smooth, sandy beaches of Bournemouth. The distinct, dark shales of Kimmeridge Bay are known for one thing in particular; like the Burning Cliff of Ringstead, the strata is so saturated with kerogen (made up of 70 per cent organic material from formerly living organisms) that a 'nodding donkey' oil well has been constructed to extract it. This oil well now acts as a helpful landmark for the location.

The fossils you can find here are also similar to those around Weymouth Bay, though from personal experience I've found ammonites more commonly coming from the rocks here than at either Osmington or Ringstead. The nearby Etches Collection highlights the spectacular finds it's possible to make around this part of the coast, based around the discoveries of local fossil hunter Steve Etches. It is well worth a visit for inspiration on just how much is out there to be discovered.

As you move past Kimmeridge, you find the Jurassic strata come to a sudden end, replaced by the mostly Cretaceous overlying rock of Purbeck itself. There are still a few fossil locations around, though, such as the thin band shales of Durlston Bay and the later shell beds of Studland Bay.

Both of these areas do yield fossils and are well worth a visit in their own right, but don't expect to find the same plethora of fossils as you may have become used to down the coast. Having once spent a day trying to extract the remains of a crushed Cretaceous turtle at Durlston, only to have myself and colleagues deem it futile well after the sun set, I can report this from somewhat bitter experience.

Nevertheless, the Jurassic Coast is truly the most spectacular locality for fossil discoveries in the UK, with far too much to potentially discuss than could ever be contained within these few pages. With so much history, opportunity and wonder, there is no doubt that it has earned its place as the absolute pinnacle of fossil hunting in Britain.

Durdle Door and Lulworth Cove

As if fossils weren't enough, Dorset also boasts another of Britain's most famous geological sites, right up there with the White Cliffs of Dover and the Giant's Causeway. Even if you haven't heard its name, it's almost guaranteed you'll have seen its picture, be it in textbooks or tourism adverts (for which it has long been a poster child): the arch of Durdle Door.

Protruding from the white chalk cuttings of the Purbeck Hills is a jagged crop of grey limestone jutting out into the water, standing almost perpendicular to the tidal flow. The sheer sides are cracked with green veins as the coastal plant life clings to the walls. As it sticks into the sea, the rock stretches out into a rainbow shape, leaving a perfectly arched window to the channel. Though it might look at first like a bending finger of rock, that is certainly not how it was formed. It is not so much an extension of additional rock as it is a lot of missing rock.

Originally, the rocky headland would have been a solid wall and, at the base of the strata, where it met the sea, erosive forces began to act on the crevices in the stone. Eventually, a cave formed and, with the rock being relatively thin, the waves managed to power through to the other side, creating a small archway close to the water line. Once exposed, the inner rock was more vulnerable to weathering as the winds and sea channelled through it, grinding away the walls and widening the gap bit by bit. After thousands of years of erosion, the archway as we know it was complete.

'Complete' is a rather inaccurate description, however, as the story will not stop here. The archway is still being eroded and, one day, the rock will wear too thin, too fragile to support itself, and the arch will collapse into the water, leaving behind the headland on one side, and a lonely pillar of rock on the other. This standing remnant is known as a stack and it too will one day be worn away to collapse by the erosive powers of the sea and air.

This process has happened countless times before, resulting in the many stacks you can see around the coast today. A treasured World Heritage site, the integrity of the arch at Durdle Door is monitored regularly by UNESCO. Sadly, though, being listed as important doesn't mean it can be preserved for ever, as demonstrated by a similarly famous archway in Malta, the Azure Window, which succumbed to natural forces and collapsed entirely in 2017.

One thing often missed in the explanation of Durdle Door was how the area was susceptible to this irregular erosion in the first place. Incredibly, this coastline is linked with the growth of the Alps, more than five hundred miles away. This mountain range was formed following massive tectonic activity in Europe, towards the start of the Cenozoic, around 60 million years ago. These extreme forces created a large, undulating fold system of which the coastline near Weymouth is a part. We call this system the Lulworth Crumple, and its effects can be best seen at another famous geological site not far away.

Just over a mile from Durdle Door is the fantastically picturesque Lulworth Cove. Like the arch, this section was altered by the crumple, shifting a wall of hardened Portland Limestone to face the waves, protecting softer chalk strata behind. However, all it took was one gap in that defence for the erosion to hit the chalk, and hit hard. The waves were quickly able to erode the soft rock, but not the hard limestone. The result is a beautifully round bay with a sturdy gateway to the channel. Now a hotspot for tourists, Lulworth Cove is one of the most idyllic-looking bays in Britain.

Not to be left out of the fossil action, just east of the cove is an impressive display of preserved tree bases. These are the remains of lagoonal forests that grew as the Jurassic seas retreated 140 million years ago. These fossilised stumps, similar to modern-day Monkey Puzzle trees, are exceptionally complete. At the time of writing, however, they sadly cannot be accessed due to a landslip in the region, and it's unsure whether they will become reachable again. Hopefully, in time, they will be safely exposed once more, and the Jurassic Coast can reclaim another gem in its already rather excessive crown.

Sandown

The Jurassic Coast may be the most prosperous grounds for fossils in the country, but it is not the only place with palaeontological clout on the south coast. We are ending our journey through the country off the mainland on the Isle of Wight, an area that has earned the nickname the 'Dinosaur Isle'.

To explore this reputation on the island, you'll be immediately guided to the museum of that name in Sandown on the south-east coast. Its placement here no coincidence, as the beaches to the north are rich in fossils of giant reptiles. Up the shore you'll see the tall, white strata of Culver Cliff, but we are specifically looking at the slumping cliffs of grey rock between the flat beaches and chalk cliffs. This rock is part of the Wealden formation, Cretaceous in age and similar to the strata seen in places like Smokejack Clay Pit (see p. 180).

Dinosaur bones are more common here than in most places in the UK, and can often be found washed up on the shore free from any matrix. Their distinctive black colour helps them to stand out against the shore line, and you should be sure to keep an eye out for that slight honeycomb texture that so often gives away a bone. As with the marine reptile deposits, vertebrates are the most common sections discovered, with one of the most common species being *Mantellisaurus* (a dinosaur extremely similar looking, and with a similar lifestyle, to *Iguanodon*).

Another dinosaur you can discover here is reminiscent of the *Scelidosaurus* of Charmouth (see p.214). A quadrupedal herbivore covered in armoured plating, this is *Polacanthus*. A few million years of evolution down the line and this animal was firmly in the group known as the ankylosaurs. A popular member of this family is *Ankylosaurus*, an eight-tonne, eight-metre-long beast with a heavy club at the end of its tail, likely used for defence against large theropods like *T. rex*. This species lived much later in the Cretaceous, however, and only in North America, a newly formed ocean away from *Polacanthus*.

Like the other ankylosaur we've previously discussed, *Hylaeosaurus*, the Isle of Wight ankylosaur didn't have a club tail and was much smaller, though it did have spiked scutes (small plates of bone armour), much larger than any on its Jurassic ancestors. One interesting feature that *Polacanthus* showed was a fusing of the armour plating above the hip, giving it a kind of protective saddle. Though we know much about the body armour of this species, relatively little is known about the head or limbs due to a lack of material.

A question that inevitably follows is: if these dinosaurs were armoured, what were they protecting themselves from? During the 1980s and 90s, the cliffs to the south provided answers to that question when they revealed skull and body material with all the hallmarks of belonging to a large theropod dinosaur. Named *Neovenator*, its huge, clawed hands and elevated nasal crests on the skull suggested it was part of a family called the Allosauroidea.

This group of dinosaurs lived all around the world, from the famous predator of Jurassic North America, *Allosaurus*, to the shark-toothed African *Carcharodontosaurus*, and the huge South American *Giganotosaurus*. As with all British dinosaurs, our *Neovenator* was not one of these giants, although measuring about 7.5 metres in length still makes it one of the largest carnivores the UK has ever seen. A full skeletal reconstruction of this beast can be seen in the Dinosaur Isle museum in Sandown.

The Dinosaur Isle museum has been built specifically to take on the shape of a large pterosaur, and they wouldn't have done this without good reason; pterosaur material has also come from these Cretaceous cliffs. One of the most exciting of these was revealed in 2020, as the remains of a new species of pterosaur were discovered at Sandown. Like the previous pterosaurs we've seen (p.213), it had the same odd wing structure and lightly built skeleton, but the skull notably featured a large display crest, linking it with the Tapjarid pterosaurs from around the world (the group named for the famously bizarre South American *Tapejara*, which sported an incredible towering fin-crest on its head).

The new genus, named *Wightia* in honour of the island, was much larger than the *Dimorphodon* of the Jurassic. They may not have been dinosaurs but, in typical Mesozoic style, the pterosaurs still exploded in size across their evolution. As the dinosaurs were the largest to walk the earth, the pterosaurs were the largest animals to fly. The biggest of them is thought to have been *Hatzegopteryx*, with a wingspan of up to twelve metres. For comparison, that's about the same as a Eurofighter Typhoon military jet, and five metres more than the largest known flying bird, *Pelagornis* (a giant South Carolina seabird from 25 million years ago).

The Isle of Wight certainly does earn its palaeontological reputation, and we've only covered one side of it so far. There's even more to see over on the western shores of the island, where our journey will conclude.

Isle of Wight AONB

The final sites highlighted in this book are aptly named: the Isle of Wight Area of Outstanding Natural Beauty. Like the sites on the east coast of the island, this is a place known for incredible Cretaceous discoveries.

To the north of this beautiful coastline are the island's iconic geological features, the chalk stacks of the Needles, but we are going to start at the southern end, between Atherfield and Brighstone. Having focused on the glorious reptile finds of the island so much already, it is worth noting that invertebrates are also abundant here, and this part of the island is the best place to find crustaceans, in the excitingly named 'Lobster Beds'.

The most commonly found crustaceans here belong to the genus *Meyeria*. These are the fossils that give the formation its name, even though, despite their appearance, they are not true lobsters at all. However, *Meyeria* does belong to the grouping known as the decapods, the same order of crustaceans as lobsters and crabs— named for having ten appendages, but these are unique animals, now all long extinct.

The knobbly-textured dark carapaces of these animals are often easy to spot protruding from the hazy grey or yellow colour of most of the matrix they are found in, and they are usually found in a shrimp-like position, their tails curled around underneath their bodies. This thin layer of greensand is frequently covered and uncovered by the falling cliffs, so finding crustacean remains here isn't always reliable, but it's well worth checking out, as they're more abundant and well preserved here than most Mesozoic crustaceans in the UK.

Further up the coast you reach Hanover Point, and a return to those fossil-hunting fan favourites, the dinosaurs. Some of the most celebrated finds from here are the casts of footprints regularly found on the shore. Unlike the classic depressions of footprints, these are three-dimensional casts regularly free of the bedrock, giving them the look of having been cut out of the rock with a dino-foot cookie-cutter. The most common impressions can be more than sixty centimetres across and belong to dinosaurs similar to *Iguanodon* (if not *Iguanodon* itself).

Bone fragments can also emerge from the cliffs here, though most are fragmentary and hard to specifically identify as belonging to any one species. The greensand rocks here are still Cretaceous in age, and large bones can quickly be attributed to dinosaurs, though some other reptile remains, like turtles, also can be found here before you reach some of the chalk exposures and the classic marine fossils we've discussed previously.

Tantalisingly there have been finds of toe bones of an unidentified sauropod dinosaur washed up around these shores. With this and the mysterious *Duriatitan* across the waters in Dorset, it could be only a matter of time before somebody uncovers something truly enormous from the ancient UK strata.

One of the more spectacular finds over the past few years was the discovery of over fifty dinosaur bones on a beach near Brighstone. Examination of these bones resulted in the naming of not one but two new species of spinosaurid dinosaur (similar to *Baryonyx*) in 2021. These large fish-eaters were given the names *Ceratosuchops inferodios* and *Riparovenator milnerae*, the former translating to the suitably dramatic title of 'Horned Crocodile-faced Hell Heron'.

The final discovery to highlight in this book is interesting in that I cannot reveal the exact location it was found. This is the case of multiple discoveries on the Isle of Wight that have been deemed especially important, in order to protect them from being stormed by tourists. If any animal discovery could inspire a fossil gold rush, it was this one.

In 1995, a small claw was discovered on the island and taken to the Museum of Geology in Sandown (the former name of Dinosaur Isle). Quickly identifying it as significant, a project was launched in secret to excavate the area. It was long work, but five years after that first discovery, the fossils recovered were formally described. This was *Eotyrannus*, Britain's only known tyrannosaur.

Unlike its famous cousin from the Badlands of the USA, the British tyrannosaur wasn't a giant. *Eotyrannus* was about 4.5 metres in length and 1.5 metres tall, measuring about one-third of the size of *T. rex*. Even so, those distinctive tyrannosaur teeth show that this animal was a hunter. They have the classical horror-style look of being large and conical with a serrated edge, perfect for taking chunks out of their prey.

The tyrannosaurs were a much larger and more diverse group than simply *Tyrannosaurus rex* alone. So rich is their evolutionary history that the difference in time between the *Eotyrannus* and *T. rex* actually isn't too far off the difference in time from *T. rex* to now (about 66 million years). Relatives have been found all over the world, some with various unique features, such as the notable crest of the Asian species *Guanlong*, but they were all part of that most famous of palaeontological groups. The UK is a country with an incredible palaeontological heritage, and this predator of the Wealden group being part of that royal family of dinosaurs is just the cherry on top.

Fossil Preparation

You're back from the field with a healthy collection of new finds in your bag – what comes next? There's quite a difference between the fossils fresh from the beach and those pristine specimens on display in museum cases. Bridging that gap is the world of fossil preparation.

Many of the fossils you'll have collected will have come from coastal sites, many from the wash of the shore itself. Once collected, these fossils will begin to dry out, the water evaporating but leaving behind crystals of sea salt. Fossils are more similar to us than you might realise; too much salt is really quite bad for them. And thus, the best first step for a lot of fossils is to give them a bath.

Thankfully this process doesn't require anything more exotic than regular tap water to soak them in. The amount of time this takes can vary depending on the size and quantity of the fossils, and where they were collected (recently fallen material will need less than something that has been sitting in the tide for days). Replace the water every now and then to remove that salt and after a few days they should be stable (nothing about fossil preparing is particularly fast, unfortunately).

This technique isn't ideal for all fossils, as delicate specimens in mudstones and siltstones may dissolve away completely if submerged like this, and their best bet for survival is in proper storage (see the next section). Alternatively, for some sturdy fossils preserved in clays, this may well be the only prepping needed, as the water makes the clay malleable enough to easily rub away from the fossil.

This brings us to the next step in prep work, which can be done along with the soaking process: removing the excess matrix from the fossils. After all, hammers aren't exactly the most precise tools of the trade, and it's not a great idea to try and get fossils out perfectly out in the field; they're going to come with some of the rock attached, and now in a controlled environment with better kit and more time, you can try to remove it.

Specialist tools do exist for this kind of work and can be purchased from geological kit suppliers, but so long as you're sensible and safe, something like a field knife will often do the trick as well. Some surprisingly effective tools for softer rocks are old toothbrushes, which are excellent at cleaning up fossils, as are the ultrasonic baths usually employed for cleaning jewellery.

The most specialist tools of all are air scribes, special pens which use compressed air to remove rock carefully and precisely. If you've ever seen fossil specimens in museums with small whitened lines around them, those are the traces of the air-scribe work. Removing rock like this is an extremely slow and laborious process, one which takes many hours to achieve and much training beforehand, but the results can be incredible. Even so, this is not an investment of time or money I'd recommend for any but the most dedicated of fossil hunters.

One technique you may also have heard of is 'acid preparation'. Many fossils are preserved in limestone, which will dissolve away when exposed to dilute acetic acid (the same acid in vinegar). For the average fossil hunter, this technique is frankly often more effort than it's worth. It can take weeks, if not months, to work fully, meaning you need to set up and monitor it over that time, and it only works on specific fossil types (and even for those it can leave the fossil fragile and in need of extra care).

But there are occasions when this technique can shine for the regular fossil hunter, and that's in revealing micro fossils. Cave fissure fills (like those in Aust) have jumbled remains all bundled together. Dissolving these bone bed chunks can reveal hidden gems like teeth and scales you wouldn't have known were hidden within.

Even when diluted, though, working with acid can be hazardous, so it should only be attempted with sufficient extra research to ensure that it's being conducted in a safe and responsible manner.

Before moving on, it's worth noting that this is a very rapid summary of some of the major preparation techniques you might undertake at home. Every fossil specimen is unique and the steps taken to prepare them are dependent on the fossil type, mode of preservation, matrix type, time out of the ground, as well as many other factors. Preparation isn't just a side note on a hobby, for many it's a full-time job requiring years of experience, performed by a group of people who often don't get the acknowledgement they deserve for the incredible work they do.

Storage and Care

Fossils are rocks. Rocks are tough. Therefore, fossils are tough and I can just throw them anywhere. This is the thinking that has led to the demise of countless fossils over the years. Don't let it happen to yours. Fossils are the lowest maintenance pets you'll ever have, so long as you get the basics right to start with.

When thinking about where to keep your fossils, there are a few things to keep in mind: relative humidity, abrasions, lighting and temperature. A lot of these things are linked, and can be summed up under the first key rule: don't keep your fossils outside.

When it comes to keeping fossils, you need to think long term. Stored outside, you might not notice anything wrong for a year or more, but it will take a toll. The temperature fluctuations expand and shrink your specimen, fracturing the rigid rock. Humidity changes only makes this process more extreme, as the specimen constantly takes in and loses water. Direct sunlight can make specimens particularly frail as well. Before you know it, your unique fossil has fractured into dust and you've managed the frankly impressive feat of killing something that's been dead for millions of years.

To be kept in one piece, fossils should be stored in a controlled environment; somewhere away from direct light where temperatures and humidity are unlikely to change.

There's nothing wrong with having them on display, just not exposed near an open window. A good rule of thumb is to consider whether you would keep bread there. Bread stored in a humid room in direct sunlight will inevitably get mouldy fairly quickly. Storing it in a cool, dry place will help it keep for longer. Thankfully you don't need to worry about having to eat fossils, and so silica gel packets, like those found in packaging, can help keep the storage humidity under control too.

Try not to lump all of your fossils together somewhere without protection, as they can do surprising amounts of damage to each other just by, for example, bumping into one another when you open their drawer. Each knock creates more micro-fractures, until one day bits start crumbling away. This can all be avoided with something as simple as a nest of tissue.

Some tissues contain acids that can damage the fossils if left unchecked. This isn't a fault with the tissues, they're just not meant to work on the long timescale necessary for fossils. If you want the collection to last, you can invest in some acid-free tissue (or plastazote if you really want to give them a good home). A key thing to look out for in gathering material is the term 'conservation grade'.

One last thing to mention in terms of fossil care is something that is the bane of so many collections, the palaeontological devil that is 'pyrite decay'. Many fossils are preserved in pyrite (such as the ammonites of Charmouth or the plant material of Sheppey) and this material, whilst pretty, can be volatile. Pyrite decay is a complex chemical process but the key thing is that it's irreversible, and the end product is larger in size than the original, so if it gets into your collection, it can make specimens explode from the inside and you might be powerless to stop it.

If you spot it beginning (a tell-tale sign being small concentrations of yellow powder around the specimens), the first thing to do is some fossil social-distancing. Pyrite decay can spread between fossils, so isolating the specimen can contain it. There is nothing that can undo the damage already done, but you can slow or stop it progressing further by ensuring it is stored somewhere with highly reduced humidity (preferably below 30 per cent). Outside of this, you may need to consult a professional fossil conservator or accept you've lost it and move it away to slowly explode in peace, taking a photo to contribute to a 'ghost collection'.

So now your fossils are prepared and safe, but there is one factor no collection is complete without – information. As someone who has spent countless hours sorting through mysterious collections in museum stores, I think I can speak for all of my curator colleagues when I say that you have no idea how important keeping information with your collections is. The basics are the most important: what is the specimen and where did you find it (physical location on the beach and stratigraphic level if you know it). Write it down, and keep it on a card with the specimen, or alongside a picture in a virtual catalogue, or both!

When it comes to information, the more the better! You can include the date you found it, your name, what was around it, is it associated with any other specimens? All this information builds up a complete picture and can be useful for anyone who might study your discoveries one day.

Though it may be repetitious, it really is crucial to think in larger time scales for fossils. When writing a date, for instance, put all four numbers of the year; it might sound ridiculous but you'd be surprised. When curating collections of amateur hunters at Bristol Museum, finding a specimen labelled 'Collected in '76' doesn't mean too much for an institution that has existed since 1823. Which '76? Think big, as you never know where your fossils could one day end up, and there's nothing museums love more than a well-curated collection.

By following all of these steps, you may well find yourself with a collection on your hands. This is a wonderful thing shared by many science enthusiasts the world over, but if you own a collection, it's good to understand some of the facts of how this affects science.

One of the stipulations of scientific research is that data must be accessible for others to use in their own work, essentially a way of fact checking the work (results are repeatable). Because of this, for the most part private collections cannot be used in regular published scientific study.

Therefore, it's good practice to report finds you suspect to be important. Avoid pushing them on the shady fossil trading markets where they end up lost in private collections, never to be seen again. Most palaeontologists have a loathing for the private fossil trade and all the specimens lost to it; there are whole incredible new species that the world doesn't know about because they're locked behind someone's closed doors. Integral to fossil hunting as a hobby is going out, exploring and discovering things yourself. You don't get the same rush of a remarkable discovery in the wild when you buy a fossil you had nothing to do with finding.

A good thing to do with special fossils is to donate them to museums which may take them on into their stores where they are well looked after and accessible to all scientists, though you certainly shouldn't feel the need to do this with literally *all* your finds; museum storerooms around the country are already filled to bursting point with specimens and, without funding or support, they simply can't always cope with requests. Museum folk are some of the loveliest people and, if you reach out to them because you suspect you've found something great, they'll happily help you out (just be respectful and patient, as they do get a lot of enquiries!).

Urban Palaeontology

It's only natural that most of the places you can go to hunt for fossils are in out-of-the-way locations, often fairly remote, usually along the coastline, but the vast majority of people in Britain live in cities, with estimates that 80 per cent of the population live in urban areas. Vast metropolitan expanses of London may seem about as far away as you can get from the near-wilderness feel of some of the places we've covered, but the odds are that you might pass more fossils on a day of walking through a city than you would on a day at the beach, even if you don't always notice it. This is 'urban palaeontology', and it is an inevitable by-product of our cities.

One such example is the Cabot Circus shopping complex right in the centre of Bristol. Sections of the shopping-centre perimeter are composed of huge slabs of white Portland limestone, covered in small divots and holes. Hundreds of people commute past them every day, but few stop for a closer look.

The indents have very distinctive shapes, many of them the unmistakable spirals of turret-shelled gastropods, and classic clam-shaped bivalves. All it takes is a momentary glance and suddenly it becomes obvious; every single impression on the wall shows where a marine invertebrate once lay embedded on the Jurassic sea floor. It's an entire preserved ecosystem turned on its side and now propping up a department store.

Once you begin to take notice of such things, it becomes impossible to not see them everywhere, and you start to realise just how much palaeontology is around you. We rely on fossiliferous rocks so much that they're inescapable, and fossils, or at least fragments of them, turn up more often than not.

This is far from a new phenomenon either. In Worcester Cathedral lies the tomb of King John (famous signer of the Magna Carta and villain of Robin Hood mythology). His likeness is carved into a dark brown rock, covered in yellow and silver circles, clearly the cross-sections of oyster-like fossils, and there are literally thousands of them.

Seeing as King John died in 1216, long before ideas of the deep past and fossilisation were formed in the minds of natural philosophers (a profession we now refer to as a scientist), you have to wonder what the original architects made of their materials, how they interpreted what these patterns may have been, and whether they could have comprehended the incredible truth.

Probably the most common producer of urban palaeontological opportunities is limestone, a rock we love to use in our buildings for its aesthetically pleasing nature. But, as we've explained before, limestone is composed of those carbonate oozes on the ancient sea floor, made up predominantly of the decaying bodies of ancient organisms. Even with the high probability of finding fragments of seashells within it, you could say that, technically, the entire substance is a fossil of sorts, and though it is perhaps a little bleak to know that the rock used in many beautiful buildings (like those in the Roman city of Bath) is in fact made up of millions of dead organisms, it does certainly add a layer of scientific intrigue. Even the Houses of Parliament are clad in Permian limestone from Yorkshire, containing more than their fair share of shelly fragments.

More than simply buildings, however, fossils can be found underfoot often enough, and I'm not referring to fossils buried beneath the surface, but the surface itself. Though concrete and asphalt dominate major metropolitan areas, it's still not unusual to find sedimentary paving slabs in public areas of towns and cities.

Such a resource of fossil-spotting opportunities inspired the creation of the group 'London Pavement Geology' (www. londonpavementgeology.co.uk) by Dave Wallis and Ruth Siddal. This is an online database of the unique but often ignored geological stories that surround us. As it has grown, it has moved past just pavements to incorporate all kinds of structures and the fossils or geological features within. It's interesting to look up your local area to see what you might find is right on your doorstep and, accepting user submissions, you can even add your own urban palaeontological discoveries for others to enjoy.

Unlike the other places in this book, this is palaeontology not restricted to any one area, and more than just the UK, this is a global phenomenon. Bivalves have infiltrated the Pentagon, brachiopods sit in the steps of Chichén Itzá, and crustaceans lie in the Australian Parliament House (including one complete specimen nicknamed 'Shawn the Prawn'). From personal experience, I can say some of the best nautiloid fossils I've ever seen are preserved en masse in a cross-section of the floors covering Stockholm Airport, and one of my favourite ammonite-spotting localities was a residential garden wall outside my university halls.

We construct buildings made out ancient sea floors, and live in a world formerly powered by burning fossil plants, and use our understanding of past ecosystems to predict and model how the world might look in the future, and how best to conserve it using renewable energies and technologies made possible by the wonders of modern geology. Palaeontology isn't simply a hobby of fossil hunting; you don't even need to look very hard to see that it is everywhere, and it's amazing.

Acknowledgements

Being able to put the fossils and locations in this book in the context of current exciting research was only possible thanks to having discussions with and consulting a myriad of different researchers in the palaeontology community. Their research, expertise and advice were invaluable.

Those earliest life forms and phylogenetics were explored with help of Dr Holly Betts, Dr Gareth Coleman and Dr Frankie Dunn. The famous dinosaurs were discussed with assistance from Dr Logan King and Professors Emily Rayfield and Mike Benton. Dr Nuria Melisa Morales García and Kim Chandler lent their expertise on extinct mammals, in particular the mysterious world of their earliest relatives. The larger mammal megafauna were revealed with help from the work of Dr Steven Zhang.

A great deal of information on the pterosaurs, the flying reptiles of the Mesozoic, was provided by Dr Liz Martin-Silverstone and Ben Griffin. Meanwhile, in the seas, the marine reptiles were informed greatly by the work of Dr Ben Moon and Dr Tom Stubbs, with Jack Cooper giving guidance on the sharks which swam alongside them.

Beyond the fossils themselves, descriptions of geological features and processes in this book were made possible with the consultation of volcanologist Dr Ailsa Naismith, reef expert Mike Hynes, and taphonomist Mark Stanley. Much historical and current context for the fossil world was revealed by Isla Gladstone and Debs Hutchinson, curators at the Bristol Museum & Art Gallery. And finally, the hidden world of microfossils was revealed with help from a collection of climate scientists: Dr Laura Cotton, Chloe Louise Todd and Sophie Gayne.

Many in the UK palaeo community were happy to help out by contributing knowledge of their own local sites, including Jack Lovegrove, James Rawson, Emily Keeble, Dr Bethany Allen, Ben Eagle and Emily Green.

In particular, I would like to mention my former flatmate and undergraduate colleague Dr Fiann Smithwick, whose expertise and skill in fossil hunting is unrivalled, and who taught me many of the tricks and techniques in fossil hunting and preparation (along with others who have accompanied and assisted on expeditions, including Dr Suresh Singh, Dr Jess Crumpton-Banks, Richie Jalili, Ellen MacDonald and Tim Nichols).

A great deal of thanks needs to go to the wider fossil-hunting community, whose research and contributions to online forums and sites such as the UK Fossils Network have inspired and informed many of my own fossil hunting trips over the years, certainly aiding to highlight some of the 'must-see' areas I've spoken about here.

Last but not least, this book was only possible thanks to the palaeo-patience and eternal encouragement of my parents and wider family.

Index